CHARLESTON VOICES

Charleston Voices *is an ongoing yearly series that publishes chapters based on ideas first shared at the annual Charleston Conference.*

CHARLESTON VOICES

Perspectives from the
2017 Conference

EDITED BY LARS MEYER

Published in the United States of America by
ATG LLC (Media)

DOI: http://dx.doi.org/10.3998/mpub.11281794

ISBN 978-1-941269-23-7 (paper)
ISBN 978-1-941269-24-4 (e-book)

against-the-grain.com

CONTENTS

INTRODUCTION

Lars Meyer

Following the 2017 Charleston Conference, the Charleston Conference editorial team analyzed session attendance counts, survey feedback from conference attendees, and social media mentions.[1] Based on that analysis, we reached out to presenters and asked them to expand their presentations into a chapter for inclusion in the first volume of *Charleston Voices*.

The authors contributing to *Charleston Voices* represent library, publisher, vendor, technology, and professional association perspectives. The topics they address vary widely and are typical of the issues and challenges faced by anyone working to acquire and make available library resources or scholarly content. Improving access to content and managing resources are two recurring themes in the chapters.

The chapters in *Charleston Voices* fall into three broad subjects: the changing nature of library collections and services, standards, and assessment.

THE CHANGING NATURE OF LIBRARY COLLECTIONS AND SERVICES

Lorrie McAllister and Shari Laster, in "The Future of Print in the Open Stacks," explore novel approaches to determining which books to put where in a library based on taking a deliberate design approach.

---

1. The Charleston Conference editorial team consists of Katina Strauch, Tom Gilson, Leah Hinds, Matthew Ismail, and Lars Meyer.

In "Communicating Collections to Stakeholders: The Good, The Bad, And The Spreadsheets," Sarah McClung, Karen Gau, Beth Blanton-Kent, and Glenn Johnson-Grau review strategies for communicating collection development decisions. They note the importance of developing an overall strategy that encompasses different communication approaches for different audiences.

Libraries have begun to respond to the rising cost of textbooks. Jeanne Hoover and Cynthia Shirkey in "The Past is Prologue: Telling Our Stories About Textbook Affordability Programs" and Serin Anderson and Suzan Parker in "A Tale of Two Textbook Programs: Seeking A Sustainable Model for Textbook Access in Academic Libraries" examine the library's role in supporting student success by acquiring textbooks. They provide an overview of different strategies and also consider the complementary role of open educational resources (OER) initiatives.

As libraries rethink which part of their collections to keep on site and how to make library spaces responsive to user needs, libraries are examining how their services also need to change. Barbara G. Tierney and Linda K. Colding in "Reimagining Research Services as Part of Major Academic Library Renovations or Other Changes: A Tale of Two Research Departments (University of Central Florida and Florida Gulf Coast University)" examine how services at two universities with significantly different enrollments have evolved.

STANDARDS

Formal, internationally recognized standards help libraries and publishers succeed. In "COUNTER: Release 5 of the Code of Practice," Lorraine Estelle reviews the benefits of the forthcoming release, expected January 2019. The fifth release will make it easier for publishers and providers to achieve compliance in reporting electronic resource usage.

Users of electronic resources regularly encounter barriers to access. Todd Carpenter, Ann Gabriel, Robert Kelshian, and Don Hemparian in "Streamlining Access to Content in a One-Click World: RA21 Pilots Balance Researcher Productivity and User Privacy" review the work that has been completed toward developing an open standard aimed at providing users "access to all content from any location on any device of their choosing" while also respectful of privacy.

ASSESSMENT

Libraries and publishers are interested in knowing *which* library resources are used. There is also growing interest in learning more about *how* resources are used. In "Statistical Analysis, Data Visualization, and Business Intelligence Tools for Electronic Resources in Academic Libraries," Cheng Cheng, Tracy Gilmore, Colleen Lougen, and Connie Stovall explore how to use a variety of approaches and tools to inform evidence-based decision making when analyzing expenditures or planning budgets.

Helen Adey, Jesse Koennecke, and Andrea Eastman-Mullins explore the challenges associated with determining how users value, not just use, resources in "Impact Analytics: Empowering Libraries to Evaluate the Meaningful Use of E-Resources." They review the outcomes of working on two respective research projects with a publisher and a student-led business intelligence class project.

In "Data-Driven Decision Making for Electronic Resources," Priya Shenoy, Teri Koch, and Laura Krossner compare a local methodology for analyzing the use and cost of electronic resources against the findings of a survey of practices at other libraries.

Analyzing the impact of open access publications is explored in "Wide Open or Just Ajar? Evaluating Real User Metrics in Open Access." Amy Brand, Hillary Corbett, Byron Russell, and Charles Watkinson consider the challenges associated with collecting, managing, and assessing usage data from three standpoints: authors, libraries, and funders, and reflect on how the use of open access articles outside of academia presents assessment challenges.

The chapters in this volume address emerging and continuing concerns for libraries and publishers and point to novel approaches and practices aimed at improving the publication, management, and use of scholarly resources. Going forward, *Charleston Voices* will continue to publish chapters based on ideas first shared at the annual Charleston Conference.

THE FUTURE OF PRINT
IN OPEN STACKS

Lorrie McAllister
Associate University Librarian for Collections & Strategy,
Arizona State University, lorrie.mcallister@asu.edu

Shari Laster
Head, Open Stack Collections, Arizona State University,
shari.laster@asu.edu

ABSTRACT

Arizona State University is embracing new ways of thinking about how open stacks can make books active objects of engagement for a new generation of students, rather than risk becoming mere backdrops for study spaces. By taking a deliberate design approach to answering the question of "which books, where?," ASU Library seeks to position print collections as an engagement mechanism. This chapter presents the transformative potential of open stacks, along with planning for access, assessment, and inclusive engagement. The authors describe how ASU Library is using a major library renovation project as a catalyst to explore these ideas, and propose a pathway to developing shared solutions for more effective use of library collections.

INTRODUCTION

At the 2017 Charleston Conference, Jim O'Donnell, university librarian at Arizona State University (ASU), set forward "The Future of Print in Open Stacks: A Proposal," envisioning a bright future for the use of printed books in libraries. He argued that print books have become pleasant furnishings and backdrops for quiet study within the open stacks of academic libraries and declared that a glorious future for print books demands strategy.[1] At ASU, we are embracing new ways of thinking about how our open stacks can make books active objects of engagement for a new generation of students,

---

1. See: http://www.youtube.com/watch?v=Go4GJCYCLqk

rather than risk becoming mere backdrops for study spaces. The tradition of direct access to printed books in libraries is foundational to invigorating user engagement with print. Therefore, we aim to position the open stacks as engagement mechanism, taking a deliberate design approach to *which* books we place *where* so that users may interact with them.

O'Donnell, along with Lorrie McAllister, associate university librarian at ASU, introduced a collaboratively authored whitepaper, "The Future of the Academic Library Print Collection: A Space for Engagement,"[2] which was written with input from faculty members and information professionals from several academic research institutions to inspire academic libraries to rethink print collections as vital tools for inquiry and engagement. The white paper, made possible by support from the Andrew W. Mellon Foundation, outlines many issues and challenges facing academic libraries regarding print collections. In this chapter, we highlight a few in particular that we feel are worthy of expansion and further study with regard to O'Donnell's Charleston proposal. We also provide an update regarding how ASU plans to employ these new ideas to address our local context.

The New Open Stacks

At ASU Library, we believe that our open stacks are not just mechanisms for collection storage, but also have the potential to transform scholarship, education, and our communities by engaging people with information. This approach necessitates examining the relationship of academic libraries to our users, looking at ways to change the traditional power dynamics of institutional collecting to develop a more democratic and inclusive approach. Government entities, to achieve more democratic solutions, often use engagement as a methodology to involve citizens in the processes of governance. In this sense, engagement is essentially a form of participation, and consultation, or the ascertaining of opinions, lies at the heart of all forms of engagement (Stewart 2009, 9). The American Library Association has acknowledged equity, diversity, and inclusion as fundamental values for library practice.[3] By innovating, assessing, and innovating again toward more inclusive practices, academic libraries may be able to incorporate participatory processes that aim to promote shared governance and greater community engagement, which should in turn inform the ongoing curation of academic library collections.

---

2. Available for download at: https://lib.asu.edu/futureprint
3. See: http://www.ala.org/advocacy/diversity

The 2017 white paper identified five primary goals for shaping the future of print collections:

> First . . . we must take a deliberate and consciously chosen approach to print collection management. Second, we are committed to the fostering of information literacy broadly speaking and print literacy specifically. Third, we seek new curation approaches to ensure that our libraries reflect the full range and nuance of global cultures, past and present. Fourth, we propose strategies (and ways of devising further strategies) to allow academic libraries to work at a network level, accommodating a larger population of students and scholars than in the past. . . . Finally, we look to extend the reach of academic libraries to engage with the communities surrounding them as a way of realizing the commitments to inclusiveness that animate our institutions today. (Arizona State University Library 2017, 7)

The word *curation* is raised in the whitepaper and in this writing to call attention to print lifecycle management as an active endeavor, in all of its various meanings. Johnson articulates the challenges of using the word *curation*, which is used in different ways by different audiences. She describes three ways to interpret curation: as the act of selection and acquiring, as exhibition-making, and as the act of sustaining a collection (Johnson 2014). We view curation of the new open stacks as an opportunity to design print with screen engagement and online discovery in mind. The Digital Curation Centre defines digital curation as active management for "maintaining, preserving and adding value to digital research data throughout its lifecycle."[4] We use the term *curation* to describe a planned, iterative series of interventions to define, create, refine, and present a grouping of materials for a specified purpose. Using a digital collections framework for print resources asks that we actively manage our stacks, rather than allowing them to simply accrete through various disconnected selection mechanisms until a particular range is full, then weed or deaccession books when space runs out.

ASU Library is using participatory methodologies to move our print curation away from hierarchical institutional decision making toward a more user-engaged, democratic, and inclusive approach to designing the stacks. This approach is in alignment with the library's overall strategic direction. As

---

4. See: http://www.dcc.ac.uk/digital-curation/what-digital-curation

McAllister has previously articulated, "In taking community needs into account, we can demonstrate the relevance of the library to its communities while serving the greater public good and fostering a positive relationship between academia and the public at large. This approach suits ASU's interest in assuming fundamental responsibility for the economic, social, cultural, and overall health of the communities it serves" (McAllister and Adams 2018, 33). The ASU Charter directs us to measure our efforts in terms of inclusiveness and success, to advance research for the common good, and to responsibly serve the economic, social, cultural, and overall health of our communities.[5] For the library, the charter is a clear directive to examine how everything we do models these principles. By articulating the design of our collections as a service to advance engagement, learning, knowledge creation, and the common good, we place collections in the same universe of possibility as our other initiatives and programs.

In his plenary talk, O'Donnell stated: "We're inventing a new generation of service." He suggests that using a fresh and thoughtful approach to building print collections will change academic library services as we know them today. Information is powerful and transformational only if it is accessible, and in order to make our over four million print books accessible alongside millions of online resources, we have some challenges to overcome in our discovery and fulfillment services. Likewise, we aim to transform our open stacks into browsable collections in which to discover and interact with previously undiscovered sources of information. O'Donnell articulates that the overarching goal of our efforts is to "invent new ways to make the print book in the modern research library exciting and visible and engaging for our students." We believe this necessitates new methodologies for collection development and placement of books in libraries. Thus, we propose a revision to the traditional notion of "open stacks."

At ASU Library, the Open Stack Collections unit has responsibility for general collections, including reference works and government documents, both those shelved in open stacks and those held at our high-density storage facility, and openly licensed digital collections, including open educational resources (OER) and government information. The open stacks as a service concept invoke the spirit of academic libraries as upholding the principles of open access to knowledge and inspiration for the campus and communities they serve (McAllister and Laster 2018, 424). Of course, all who enter our buildings are welcomed to access

---

5. See: https://president.asu.edu/about/asucharter

books on shelves. However, with the Open Education movement reaching its 18th year, we hope to use our open stack efforts as an opportunity and means to engage people and, ultimately, to promote inquiry and improve education. To accomplish this, we are taking a purposeful, participatory, and strategic approach to decision making about the selection of print books and the disposition of them to open shelving in a library or to off-site storage facilities.

Major renovations of academic library buildings often result in the movement of collections off site, and the subsequent reduction of print books in those buildings in favor of expanded spaces for library users. ASU is no exception. Hayden Library, a 252,670-square-foot library located at the center of ASU's Tempe campus, serves over 50,000 students enrolled in residential programs. A comprehensive renovation project provides the motivation for exploring how we can transform the collections in this space. At the Hayden Library groundbreaking, O'Donnell remarked that "libraries are books, and much, much more beside. Libraries are central to the educational enterprise, the critical link connecting students to the university and to the world of knowledge."[6] As we reduce our print collections footprint in the new space to expand classroom and study space, we are taking advantage of the opportunity to think flexibly and to design the 21st-century library so that space and collections have a harmonious relationship that is adaptable to changes in the local context, as activities, interests, expectations, and skills of the people who use our libraries shift over time. As part of our design agenda, we are also seizing this opportunity to transform the accessibility of our spaces and collections. This includes the physical accessibility of our building, furniture, and collections, as well as a focus on making information services easier to access and more transparent.

In higher education, access to print books is often taken for granted, along with the requisite skills for engaging with content in these works. While engagement with print is often overlooked in the pressing need to improve information skills for digital environments and contexts, there are reasons to use print books. Learning how to navigate content in a physical book and identify visual cues evident from inspecting an object are helpful strategies for working with this format. The characteristics of the physical form of a print object may themselves be

---

6. See: https://asunow.asu.edu/20180525-sun-devil-life-asu-groundbreaking-hayden-library-tower

of interest and value, including its weight, form, and structure, and interacting with a physical format can hold a reader's attention in different ways.

Collections may also be used as pedagogical tools and sites of critical discourse. They prompt questions like: Who collects and why? What's missing? How does format of the information resource matter? By surfacing the opportunity to open these questions for discussion and conversation, the academic library serves as educator, encouraging learners to adopt a critical lens to ways in which content can be aggregated and presented. In adopting a deliberate design methodology for our print collections, we hope to produce stronger and more engaging collections that will promote more effective use of the library, while extending the ways in which we fulfill our pedagogical mission.

Access and Assessment

When planning for access, enabling discovery and request fulfillment for materials is key. Libraries have used open stacks to provide opportunities for discovery for many years. With the proliferation of digital content, the use of discovery layer search interfaces has taken the place of browsing at the stacks. Off-site, high-density storage facilities may be ideal locations for books, as they are climate-controlled secure environments that will ensure these materials are preserved over the long term. They also have reliable access mechanisms that allow staff to pinpoint item locations, allowing for quick retrieval of print resources. These facilities, then, serve as fulfillment centers for collections, serving to connect people with the books they request. They are optimized for access. However, the books in off-site storage are undiscoverable without online library interfaces (Schechtman 2018). While commercial library discovery tools seek to replicate the experience of searching for digital content, they have yet to succeed in placing digital and tangible formats on equal footing, and in some ways have not substantially progressed beyond online public access catalog functions developed decades ago (Lynema, Lown, and Woodbury 2012).

Assessment of collections often focuses on usage, with circulation as the primary, and sometimes exclusive, data point for determining the extent to which current collections meet user needs (Knievel, Wicht, and Connaway 2006, 36). We posit that this approach can disadvantage many users within our walls, who may not find that the books most directly in front of them inspire interest. The question again becomes, what books do we have, and where do we put them? Our data on collection usage must be understood in light of how collections are situated in the environment in which users encounter them. A collection identified for active engagement, curated with community input, and featured within a well-designed space, may inspire different uses from a collection developed for core disciplinary exploration and research, or a collection findable through the library discovery interface and delivered from a high-density storage facility.

In developing a data-driven approach to print curation, which includes active and iterative identification and creation of engaging collections, our project also seeks to identify ways in which engagement with users provides us with data to direct future decisions. As we move beyond circulation and interlibrary loans to a more rich data environment, we can explore new ways to articulate how our communities may prefer to engage with different works, formats, and collections. At the same time we are challenged to move beyond overly reducible modes of assessment. As we assert that engagement extends beyond a single category of quantifiable transactions, we must also critically and openly reflect on the ways in which data arising from engagement enhance or inhibit a nuanced understanding of the people with whom we seek to collaborate, and adapt our actions as necessary. What we gain from this type of reframing is the creation of a heightened awareness of library practices as enacted, embodied, or realized—this is praxis in print collection management (Doherty 2005).

Inclusive Engagement

Building many of the practices explored here and in the white paper asks that we reexamine decision making about our print collections. Exploring how libraries make decisions about selection, format, arrangement, description, and retention is a first step. Working with external partners and community members will help libraries identify points in workflows in which biases influence decision makers. The Digital Library Federation's Cultural Assessment Working Group is engaged with this exploration, most recently with regard to the selection of digital content (Scates Kettler et al. 2017). We think this work has promising extensions to print collections.

As we focus on creating collections that welcome people into library spaces, we seek effective ways to involve them in processes essential to the design, selection, and display of these collections. To develop welcoming and engaging collections for all who enter our spaces, we need to rely on the knowledge and experience of a more broadly representative constituency. For our collections to become more inclusive, they must reflect the voices, perspectives, and interests of those who have been underrepresented or excluded from dominant modes of scholarly communication.

Academic library collection development policies and practices frequently result in the selection of materials that are largely congruent with existing collections. These collections can risk perpetuating dominant practices in many scholarly communities, which privilege the status quo in scope and scale of work, modes of expression, and accepted methodologies. In general, the prioritization of markers of authority still remains part of traditional library collection practices (Seeber 2018). While upending practices like these is a critical project for all libraries to engage with, we also believe that it is essential to undertake deliberate and careful consideration of how best to do so. In the intervening time we seek to transition to a model in which the materials we center for discovery and exploration both explicitly and implicitly acknowledge deficits in existing collections, as we explore how we might remediate some of the most pressing and visible inequities in our collections going forward.

In designing collections for inclusion, we also acknowledge that many ways of learning and understanding are not accounted for in how libraries organize and present materials (Olson 2011, 118). Barriers to entry include systems of classification and organization that impose meaning, expectations for access and use that demand conformance with implicit gatekeeping, and arrangement in space that places specific physical requirements on those who wish to browse and explore (Rosen 2017). We seek to address these barriers by first identifying and acknowledging them, and then working to develop mitigation strategies. Community-sourced descriptions and arrangements, virtual stacks browsing tools, and placement of library collections outside library walls are all strategies we plan to test in the months to come.

Local Context as Testbed
With generous support from the Andrew W. Mellon Foundation, ASU Library is now actively developing approaches to engaging our communities with print resources based on the vision and strategies set forward in the white paper. As of this writing, Hayden Library, the largest library on the Tempe campus of

ASU, is in the midst of a two-year renovation project. With the building empty, we have seized the opportunity to explore a zero-based budgeting approach to planning collections. We intend to select collections by determining and prioritizing what books should be situated within the library's space, rather than simply returning the books that fit from the collections previously held within the building. Throughout 2018 and 2019, staff will be working on experimental projects that set forth various engagement-oriented approaches to defining, selecting, arranging, presenting, delivering, and assessing collections. These projects extend our capacity to responsively design and produce active collections, and will inform our work on the much larger project of designing open stack collections for Hayden Library's reopening.

When Hayden Library fully reopens in 2020, we expect this space will invite learners and scholars to study, work, and interact with each other, and with our collections, services, and expertise. Our renovated Hayden Library will offer various types of space, seating, and resources intermingled as a user-centered cohesive whole, with collections designed for people to explore and use. Along with art and exhibit spaces, collections featured here will reflect intentional design of space for the needs of ASU's growing communities of learners, scholars, and visitors. Whether accessing course reserve materials, seeking and discovering information related to personal and intellectual interests, or simply passing through on the way to another destination, those who enter Hayden Library will encounter library collections in ways that we hope will engage, inspire, and welcome them.

The main floor will situate distinctive collections, including rare books and archives, alongside browsable shelves featuring materials held by these collections, in close proximity to the reading room spaces and services. The concourse will feature smaller-scale bookshelves with active, "louder" print books and digital displays highlighting complementary resources, alongside classrooms visited by masses of students each day. And the fourth floor, where most of the browsable collections will be located, will provide the setting for "quieter" volumes, alongside quiet study spaces. While "quiet," collections designed for the fourth floor will include core disciplinary works contextualized with a range of historical perspectives, major research and reference tools that are best browsed and used in print formats, and actively programmed collections that will be evaluated and redesigned over time.

Putting these design principles into action requires a careful look at the intersections between collections and operations. For example, we will need to purchase additional copies of some books to make available in specially featured, high-traffic locations, and books that are structurally sound and in good condition for general use may nevertheless be candidates for replacement with a crisp new copy. Also, relocating books on a frequent basis will require staff collaboration in developing new practices for making frequent location changes, retrieving and reshelving books in display spaces, and responding to the questions and comments that we hope will inevitably arise as a by-product of these engagement ventures.

The result of rethinking the open stacks at Hayden with a "zero-based budgeting approach" means that we are also considering how more than four million print volumes held across all of our locations contribute to engagement within Hayden Library *and* within each library on each of our campuses throughout the greater Phoenix metro area. Design choices made in support of this project will have resonance throughout our collection as a whole, and will in turn inform future directions for the experience of visitors at each of these sites.

Future Directions

At the end of O'Donnell's thought-provoking remarks at the 2017 Charleston Conference, he stated, "we also know that we cannot simply do it alone." O'Donnell is referring to the need for making a major shift in how we think about local print collections in light of their impact on our network of partner collections. Borrowing and lending services as well as shared print archiving programs may be affected. Over many decades, academic libraries have developed consortia as a response to growing financial pressures and changing expectations of space use in their buildings. Libraries have increasingly collaborated on large-scale infrastructure as they move "towards a set of services around creation, curation, and consumption of resources that are less anchored in a locally managed collection and more driven by engagement with research and learning behaviors" (Dempsey 2015, 30). Large borrowing and lending networks allow users access to even the most obscure materials located almost anywhere in the world. These same networks can also allow libraries the freedom to build local collections that provide highly curated and engaging open stack print collections. Local collections resonate with local communities because users have confidence in the network[7] to obtain all other materials needed by scholars.

Looking forward, we find there is a compelling need within the United States and beyond to pursue more directed conversations toward planning coordinated print collection development practices for the breadth of scholarly communication still published in print format. Shared print archiving networks are reaching maturity for scholarly journals and show promise for other materials such as monographs (Stambaugh and Demas 2016); still there remains a pressing need to reconcile tension between meeting local needs and addressing broad network efforts (Center for Research Libraries 2003).

Practitioners at academic libraries with shared concerns about the future of local print collections, who engage with similar concerns in their own local contexts, are well positioned to develop new strategies and nuances to the approaches that arise from our work here. Reciprocal sharing of successes, failures, and further questions to explore benefits us all: while no two contexts are exactly the same, every difference may nevertheless highlight new possibilities for those who are willing to listen and learn. To that end, we have made public a template for a case study[8] that encourages articulation of local context and the development of a strategic framework for exploring new directions for print collections. We intend to follow with our own case study and encourage others to do the same.

While the overall prospect for collecting and preserving the many products of academic work is just as tenuous as that of preserving the vast majority of digital output that represents our networked social and cultural contexts, we can work together on shared solutions for effective use of our current resources, in light of our shared responsibility to the future. Someday, we may be able to answer O'Donnell's question *"Which books, where?"*—or at the very least, better understand the implications of this question for all that academic libraries do with print.

WORKS CITED

Arizona State University Library. 2017. *The Future of the Academic Library Print Collection: A Space for Engagement.* https://repository.asu.edu/items/50125.

---

7. A collection organized by network is no longer defined according to size or physical ownership by a single entity; instead, a network in this sense is constituted by "a coordinated mix of local, external and collaborative services assembled around user needs" (Dempsey 2016).
8. See: https://lib.asu.edu/futureprint

Center for Research Libraries. 2003. *Preserving America's Print Resources: Toward a National Strategic Effort Report on the Planning Day Discussions.* http://www.crl.edu/sites/default/files/attachments/events/PAPRreport.pdf.

Dempsey, Lorcan. 2015. "Technology Co-Evolves with Organization and Behaviors." In *New Roles for the Road Ahead: Essays Commissioned for ACRL's 75th Anniversary,* edited by Nancy Allen. Association of College & Research Libraries. 22–34. http://www.ala.org/acrl/sites/ala.org.acrl/files/content/publications/whitepapers/new_roles_75th.pdf.

Dempsey, Lorcan. 2016. "The Facilitated Collection." *Lorcan Dempsey's Weblog.* January 31, 2016. http://orweblog.oclc.org/towards-the-facilitated-collection/.

Doherty, John J. 2005. "Towards Self-Reflection in Librarianship: What Is Praxis?" *Progressive Librarian* 26 (Winter 2005/2006): 11–17. http://www.progressivelibrariansguild.org/PL/PL26/011.pdf.

Johnson, Leslie. 2014. "What Could Curation Possibly Mean?" *The Signal.* March 25, 2014. https://blogs.loc.gov/thesignal/2014/03/what-could-curation-possibly-mean/.

Knievel, Jennifer E., Heather Wicht, and Lynn Silipigni Connaway. 2006. "Use of Circulation Statistics and Interlibrary Loan Data in Collection Management." *College & Research Libraries* 67, no. 1 (January): 35–49. https://doi.org/10.5860/crl.67.1.35.

Lynema, Emily, Cory Lown, and David Woodbury. 2012. "Virtual Browse: Designing User-Oriented Services for Discovery of Related Resources." *Library Trends* 61, no. 1 (September): 218–33. https://doi.org/10.1353/lib.2012.0033.

McAllister, Lorrie, and John Henry Adams. 2018. "Designing a Bright Future for Print Collections." *Against the Grain* 30, no. 3 (June): 32–33.

McAllister, Lorrie, and Shari Laster. 2018. "Open Stacks in Library Design." *Portal: Libraries and the Academy* 18, no. 3 (July): 423–29. https://doi.org/10.1353/pla.2018.0026.

O'Donnell, Jim. 2017. "The Future of Print in Open Stacks: A Proposal." Presentation, Charleston Library Conference, Charleston, SC, November 8, 2017. http://www.youtube.com/watch?v=Go4GJCYCLqk.

Olson, Hope A. 2001. "Sameness and Difference." *Library Resources & Technical Services* 45, no. 3 (July): 115–22. https://doi.org/10.5860/lrts.45n3.115.

Rosen, Stephanie. 2017. "Accessibility for Justice: Accessibility as a Tool for Promoting Justice in Librarianship." *In the Library with the Lead Pipe.* November 29, 2017. http://www.inthelibrarywiththeleadpipe.org/2017/accessibility-for-justice/.

Scates Kettler, Hannah, Lorrie A. McAllister, Kate Joranson, Susan Barrett, Greta Valentine, Jennifer Matthews, and Nora Dimmock. 2017. "Selection Task Force." *Cultural Assessment Working Group.* Last modified September 20, 2017. https://osf.io/r78ha/.

Schechtman, Kara. 2018. "How a Book Warehouse Is Changing Columbia's Library System." *Columbia Daily Spectator,* March 8, 2018. http://www.columbiaspectator.com/eye-lead/2018/03/09/how-is-a-book-warehouse-changing-columbias-library-system/.

Seeber, Kevin. 2018. "Legacy Systems." *Kevin Seeber* (blog). June 15, 2018. http://kevinseeber.com/blog/legacy-systems/.

Stambaugh, Emily, and Sam Demas. 2016. "Curating Collective Collections-Re-Inventing Shared Print: A Dynamic Service Vision for Shared Print Monographs in a Digital World." *Against the Grain* 25, no. 4 (October): 68–70. https://doi.org/10.7771/2380-176X.6591.

Stewart, Jenny. 2009. *The Dilemmas of Engagement: The Role of Consultation in Governance.* ANU Press: Acton, ACT, Australia. http://www.jstor.org/stable/j.ctt24h7p4.6.

COMMUNICATING COLLECTIONS TO STAKEHOLDERS: THE GOOD, THE BAD, AND THE SPREADSHEETS

Sarah McClung
Head of Collection Development, University of
California-San Francisco, sarah.mcclung@ucsf.edu

Karen Gau
Health Sciences Collection Librarian, Virginia
Commonwealth University, gaukh@vcu.edu

Beth Blanton-Kent
Head of Collection Development & Management,
University of Virginia, blanton@virginia.edu

Glenn Johnson-Grau
Head of Acquisitions & Collection Development, Loyola
Marymount University, gjohnson@lmu.edu

ABSTRACT

It is not uncommon for impactful collections decisions to be made behind closed doors and have an air of mystery surrounding them. Library users and non-collections librarians may be surprised to discover that a well-loved resource is no longer available or that a lesser-regarded resource was purchased instead of a resource they specifically requested. Management or non-collections librarians may fumble to answer questions about how their collections funding is being spent or how a resource is being received by users. Moments like these emphasize the importance of collections librarians effectively and thoughtfully communicating their activities and taking into consideration the impact of their decisions on these various groups, particularly when those decisions are likely to be unpopular with their communities. This chapter discusses four communication fundamentals that can be applied to improving the communication of collections decisions: establishing community relationships, building internal trust, storytelling, and communication strategy assessment. Examples are shared of ways in which four different academic libraries have implemented these fundamentals to communicate collections decisions, changes, and challenges to internal and external stakeholders.

INTRODUCTION

Collection development librarians make seemingly innumerable decisions on a daily basis. Renewals, cancellations, selection, weeding, purchasing, platform options, trials, budgeting, and more all require an extensive gathering of data and then decisiveness to ultimately meet library users' needs. When these decisions are well communicated to stakeholders, patrons can feel both valued and as though they have an understanding of why the library decided to make a change. When these decisions are not well communicated, it can be perceived as though impactful collections decisions are being made behind closed doors with an air of mystery surrounding them. Library users and non-collections librarians may be surprised to discover that a well-loved resource is no longer available or that a lesser-regarded resource was purchased instead of a resource they specifically requested. Management or non-collections librarians may fumble to answer questions about how their collections funding is being spent or how a resource is being received by users. Moments like these emphasize the importance of collections librarians effectively and thoughtfully communicating their activities and taking into consideration the impact of their decisions on these various groups, particularly when those decisions are likely to be unpopular with their communities.

Communication skills have long been considered a core competency for librarians. While no organization has released an official list of core competencies for collection development librarians specifically, American Library Association's (ALA) Core Competences of Librarianship (ALA 2009), Association for Library Collections and Technical Services' (ALCTS) Core Competencies for Acquisitions Professionals (ALCTS 2018), and North American Serials Interest Group's (NASIG) Core Competencies for Electronic Resources Librarians (NASIG 2016) all list communication and or interpersonal skills as requirements for being an effective librarian. Additionally, *Fundamentals of Collection Development and Management*, an authoritative work on the collection development role, repeatedly mentions the need for communication skills and the importance of having open communication with library users (Johnson 2018). An analysis of acquisition and collection development job announcements, a popular way to identify emerging trends and industry needs, found "communication skills" and "interpersonal skills" to be the second and third most common competencies, respectively, for collection development positions after "collection development" (Fisher 2001, 182–183). The study also demonstrated that the desirability for communication skills has increased substantially over time: in 1975, only one job posting out of the 15 analyzed had listed communication skills as a qualification; by 1999, it was mentioned in 47 out of 75 postings. Interpersonal skills had a similar increase in qualification desirability: one out of 15 postings in 1975 had listed it, but it was mentioned in 46 out of 75 postings in 1999.

Despite the clear indicators that communication is an integral part of collections work, information about the intersection of communicating decisions and library collections is lacking in the literature. Often, communication of collection development decisions is of most concern when a library undertakes large weeding or cancellation projects. While many articles have been written by librarians outlining these types of projects, few mention in detail how the decisions were communicated to their users. Perhaps relatedly, one does not have to search extensively in order to find plenty of opinion pieces published in newspapers and online about a community member's outrage at the discovery that one's library has disposed of a large number of books or unsubscribed from cherished journals. One exception found in the literature, "Cutting without Cursing: A Successful Cancellation Project," outlines how Salisbury University was able to cut nearly 20% of their journal titles without faculty outcry (Hardy, Zimmerman, and Hanscom 2016). The main reason why they were able to gain their university's support was due to the extensive communication plan they had prepared and implemented that involved the faculty at every step of the process.

While communication during a major change is imperative, collection development librarians would greatly benefit from establishing the needed communication infrastructure well before undertaking these types of large projects in order to be more effective and better received. As Jenica Rogers stated, "'In a world with insufficient money or people to make decision-making easy, [these] are your resources: your personal influence, the data you're gathering about your world, and the relationships you're building'" (2015, 71). Clear and consistent communication is key to enhancing our influence, improving the data we collect, and fostering the relationships we build. Individually, we may have little control over the reasons why we need to make changes to our collections, but we do have some level of control over our own communication. Information is not much use if it is not communicated, and collection development librarians are rich with information about what our libraries hold. We need to communicate out this information so that we can develop the authority needed for our users and partners to participate in, trust in, and be receptive to our decisions.

This chapter will discuss four communication fundamentals that can be applied to improving the communication of collections decisions: establishing community relationships, building internal trust, storytelling, and communication strategy assessment. Examples will also be shared of ways in which four different academic libraries have implemented these fundamentals to communicate collections decisions, changes, and challenges to internal and external stakeholders. For the purposes of this chapter, internal communication will refer to conveying information to your colleagues in your library and external communication will refer to conveying information to your users on your campus. Every situation and audience is unique and will call for a different communications approach; however, the four components discussed here should be universal enough to be applicable to any library project, position, or institution. These important communication concepts should be familiar, but hopefully, by giving examples of ways in which these fundamentals are being applied to collections work, the reader will be inspired to evaluate and improve collections communications at his or her own institution.

ESTABLISHING COMMUNITY RELATIONSHIPS

In past decades, when library budgets, personnel, and space were usually ample and it was possible to purchase almost anything that was deemed appropriate for an institution, librarians did not require as much input on purchase decisions. End users could expect what they needed to be available on demand due to the ability of libraries to predominately operate under the purchasing philosophy of "just in case." In this newer era of expensive electronic packages of journals, books, and videos, our collecting philosophy has largely had to shift to "just in time" and, with it, the increased need for collections librarians to not only understand but also be an active part of their user community so that purchasing decisions can be well informed and inclusive. Community relationships help all participants to be informed about collections issues and be involved in collections decisions. These types of external relationships and conversations will only increase in importance as scholarly communication continues to advance, and we must determine the best ways to move forward in developing and managing collections for the next era of scholars and scholarship.

Libraries and their attendant resources are principally perceived as a common good for the entire institution that they serve, and, as such, collections initiatives should be focused on the identification and acquisition of rich and varied resources in support of the research and teaching missions of the parent institution. As indicated in ACRL's *2016 Top Trends in Academic Libraries*, recent years have seen a significant shift in the alignment of collections philosophies, practices, and budgets toward support of institutional research and curricular mandates (ACRL 2016). Understanding those research and curricular initiatives while moving away from "just in case" collection development processes requires conversations across administrative, research, and departmental levels. "Talk about the parts that matter to them, and link them, when you can, to the things that matter to you. . . . Your network of allies can extend further than you expect, because each person you connect to is connected in a web to others" (Rogers and Wesley 2015, 72). Invitations for input should be widely distributed and all interactions must utilize inclusive language in order to promote a sense that all voices are valued. Additionally, concerted effort should be made to identify and speak to individuals involved in the interdisciplinary and emerging areas within the university so that collections librarians can not only be proactive in providing these soon-to-be-in-demand resources but also demonstrate the ability of the library to understand granular as well as institution-wide priorities. External relationships nourished by the understanding that librarians are invested in individual, departmental, school, and institutional success create a rich and rewarding environment for communicating about shared resources.

Networking, both formal and informal, must occur in order for the library's community of practice to grow and to increase its accuracy of reflecting the actual needs of its users (Trenholm and Jensen 2008). More formal methods of information exchange may occur during subject liaison and faculty meetings, instruction sessions, colloquia, and other settings. Another structured way to ensure that the library collection goals are in alignment with larger priorities is to conduct a needs assessment. While a needs assessment can be done at the individual level, it is often more useful at the broad departmental level, as this provides a glimpse at the resource requirements across specific disciplines and scholarly levels. Informal information exchanges can also provide excellent opportunities for locating key partners, learning about collections needs, communicating collections changes, and obtaining other data pertinent to collections processes and practices (Camack 2017). Resource fairs, retirement parties, award ceremonies, open office hours, and similar gatherings can all bring people together and talking. Being visible during meetings and events, no matter how unstructured, communicates to faculty and students that librarians are an active part of the community and provides further opportunities for shared and successful outcomes.

These interactions with library users provide collections librarians with a glimpse of preferences, perceptions, and patterns of use around information resources that helps them determine what resources to purchase, lease, and deaccession. Effective and mutually satisfying conversations around collections rely on a shared vision of desired outcomes, trust, and open ways of communicating. Multiple communication styles and methods are required for successful community interactions since communication among individual schools and departments is reflective of small work cultures, and effective communication for one community may not connect seamlessly with another. Learning to communicate within individual communities may require an understanding of specialized language, metaphors, stories, and past histories. Even within academic departments, communities are varied, comprised of individuals with potentially differing scholarly interests, vernaculars, goals, and opinions on the importance of different members of the population (e.g., undergraduates vs. tenured faculty members). Additionally, not every communication method, such as print, e-mail, phone calls, and in-person meetings, will provide an equal level of clarity depending on what is being communicated and who is receiving the message. This fact emphasizes the importance of using more than one method. "Communicating effectively isn't just about making sure you know who to talk to, it's also about how you do the talking. Too often I've seen library messages get lost because the medium and the audience are out of sync—even if the message itself was right on target" (Rogers and Wesley 2015, 73). Meaning is created in ongoing and sustained interactions between the library and community members and requires time, honest and thoughtful communication, and interpretative processes to arrive at shared understanding and trust (Turner and West 2006, 21).

Real-World Examples of Establishing Community Relationships

At all of the authors' institutions, librarians have found structured ways to engage with their communities directly. Faculty-led library advisory committees exist at all four campuses where members serve as both library advocates and consultants on a number of library-related topics, such as a library's strategic direction, major collections decisions, or even what hours the building should be open. The representatives on these committees at Loyola Marymount University (LMU) and the University of Virginia (UVA) are appointed by department chairs and attend meet-and-greet–type events where they receive a free lunch, hear updates about the library, and provide feedback about department-level interests. Because these faculty members are appointed, however, their levels of interest and engagement vary widely. Opportunities to sit at the table during academic planning discussions have been discovered as well. At LMU, UVA, and the University of California–San Francisco (UCSF), librarians frequently play a role in academic planning committees, which provides them with insight into new programs being developed. At Virginia Commonwealth University (VCU), the collections librarians are required to be part of the course approval process, where course reports that indicate whether or not the library collection has adequate resources on a new course topic must be submitted. Being a part of these planning processes informs proactive selection decisions as well.

Student engagement opportunities exist at several of the authors' libraries. Student advisory boards are often comprised of self-selected and enthusiastic proponents of the library. These students can be powerful advocates, introduce opportunities to integrate with the student population, surface unique concerns and feedback, and provide prospects to increase the libraries' interactions with diverse populations. A specific example from UVA is sponsoring a Hack-the-Stacks event to invite students to help develop collections from small publishers; support scholarship for diverse users; and identify and fill perceived gaps in collections supporting women, gender, and LGBTQ studies.

Fostering community engagement as a whole often requires participating in outreach activities that cross status lines. Librarians can benefit from taking the library out of the building and directly to the users. At all of the authors' institutions, teams of librarians have found such opportunities by setting up tables at well attended events; visiting departments and research groups; or attending councils, grand rounds, and journal clubs to share information on pertinent library resources and to gain a better understanding of information needs. The UVA Library has developed a structured "roadshow" format to bring the library directly to users. The roadshow is tailored to the interests of the specific department, group, or lab, and may include subject liaisons, functional specialists (e.g., copyright experts), and administrators, as well as collections team members. From the collections perspective, data is provided on what purchases have been made, how current resources are being used, and what new resources might be under consideration. After the roadshow, library staff who attended compare notes, develop strategies to respond to issues and questions, and offer opportunities for sustained conversation with the user group.

BUILDING INTERNAL TRUST

Communicating collections decisions to users is most effective when the library is conveying a single, unified message. In order to achieve that, collection development librarians must acknowledge that external stakeholders are only one part of being inclusive with collections conversations and that they also need to establish close working relationships with their library colleagues (Jones 2017). Even though colleagues may know that the collections librarian selects and purchases resources, do they really know enough about how and why decisions are made to feel confident that these decisions are the right ones? Regular and transparent communication within the library, coupled with consistent action, will not only cause colleagues to be more likely to become advocates and allies for the collections decisions that are being made, but collection development librarians can feel more confident that they are making sound purchasing and cancellation decisions.

How can a climate of trust be created? Communication plays a large role in our perceived reliability. In Hurley's 2006 article, "The Decision to Trust," one of the recommended steps to building trust between individuals is to "increase the frequency and candor of your communications" (62). Accordingly, consciously cultivating a transparent, communicative relationship with library colleagues can be essential to building long-term trust for collections-related decisions. When this openness is then supported by steady action and follow through, colleagues will acknowledge the credibility of the collections decisions that are being made. Rogers points out many ways in which our reputation and identity can set us up for success:

> You need your audience to believe in you in some way if you want them to listen to your arguments for and against. Maybe that belief comes because you're known to be trustworthy, or diligent, or detail oriented. Maybe it's because you've built a reputation as someone who always understands an issue inside and out, and who has credibility as an expert in the field. Maybe it's because you're known as the colleague who always comes through when she promises to accomplish something. . . . It doesn't matter why someone's willing to listen and believe in you, it just matters that they do. And you get that belief and willingness by building an interpersonal reputation, and an identity. Plant your flag in the values you've identified, and use them to scaffold your actions and your presence in your community and to build your credibility. (2015, 69–70)

This regular pairing of communication and action within the library can help build trust that the library collection is being shepherded along a desirable path. When colleagues are consistently updated on collections activities, regardless of how mundane the activities may seem, they gain a better sense of how and why the collection is evolving, and they have more opportunities to take part in its evolution. Not only can colleagues be compelled to become sincere advocates for the collections decisions that are being made, but collection development librarians can feel more confident that they are making sound, well-informed decisions, whether they are for everyday firm orders or for major projects like weeding and cancellations.

The implementation of a fixed communication framework can be a useful tool for fostering internal trust among collections and non-collections librarians and can make maneuvering through collections decisions a less challenging process in the long term. In fact, Georgetown University Library's Standing Committee on Collections was borne out of a cancellation task force when it was realized that creating a cross-departmental committee of librarians to discuss the collection on a regular basis could serve as an effective medium for maintaining two-way communication beyond a single project. This standing committee now encourages trust and buy-in on regular collections decisions

(Jones 2017). Being proactive and establishing a way for collections informa-tion to be communicated long before a major collection change takes place allows for more time to establish trust, to build a reputation for being reliable, for confidence in the rationales behind the decisions to strengthen, and for the strategies and nuances involved in a situation to be better understood before being tested during challenging circumstances. The following are examples of how two libraries have incorporated collections communication into their nor-mal workflows so that it occurs consistently and purposefully.

Real-World Examples of Building Internal Trust

At VCU Libraries, collection and liaison responsibilities are separate roles, so regular communication between librarians in these departments is particularly important. To facilitate an exchange of knowledge in these two areas, liaison librarians on VCU's general academic campus attend the collections librarians' monthly meetings to stay up-to-date on collections topics. At these meetings, liaison librarians learn about the library's budget, subscription additions and cancellations, consortial contracts, and other collection business. Additionally, collection librarians hold meetings with their liaison counterparts in order to stay current, and they work closely together on projects, events, and scholarship.

VCU's health sciences library has one collection librarian who works with six health sciences liaison librarians. Because of this structure, she attends the liaison meetings—instead of vice versa—in order to stay abreast of their activities across VCU's health sciences schools and the hospital. Through these monthly meetings, she learns how the liaisons are assisting faculty, students, and staff with research and instruction across its health sciences campus, and she provides highlights on collections-related activities. This allows the collection librarian to discover new areas of interest within different disciplines and answer any questions that may come up as a result of the collection updates on a regular basis. In addition to attending these monthly meetings, one-on-one meetings are set up with the health sciences liaisons at the end of each semester to discuss: (1) underutilized resources in their subject areas that can be highlighted in next semester's instruc-tion, (2) research trends across specific disciplines, (3) newly purchased resources that can be highlighted across various media, (4) e-mails or documents that merit further conversation, and (5) any collections questions the liaisons may have.

As a consequence of holding regularly scheduled meetings on both cam-puses at VCU, liaison librarians influence monograph, journal, and database purchases throughout the year, and detailed discussions about new resources or low usage numbers for existing resources occur on a routine basis, that is, not just when a momentous event requires it. The liaison librarians have also integrated the collection librarians' suggestions into their orientations, classes, newsletters, and LibGuides, and some have expressed appreciation for gaining deeper insight into collections-related activities. These meetings reflect a conscious effort to forge and maintain a strong, trusting relationship between the collection and liaison departments so that limited funds are well spent on a quality collection that will be used, and so that hard decisions can be collectively made down the road with more confidence and understanding.

At LMU, all librarians, except for the dean and associate dean, have liaison responsibilities, which includes collection development. A great deal of time and effort goes into ensuring that liaison work, despite being a "secondary responsibility" for most librarians, is fully supported and integrated into each librarian's work life. One major focus of the liaison program is to decentralize information and communications. In order to build external trust within LMU, internal trust first had to be built among the liaisons so that they can function as the megaphone that the Acquisitions & Collection Development department uses to communicate to the larger campus.

While the 24 liaison librarians have widely varied expertise and interests, few have previous collection development experience or have taken collection development courses. In order to bring these liaison librarians up to a common level of understanding to be effective in their full liaison roles, they needed to be equipped with the tools to do this part of their jobs. To ensure that librarians can effectively carry out the full range of liaison responsibilities, the collections librarians developed a formal structure for education and conversation about collections, called Pods. Each month, subject-based Pods—Humanities Pod, ArtyPod, SocioPod, and HodgePod (which includes the STEM and business liaisons)—meet so that librarians can discuss fund allocations and ordering deadlines, learn about general collections issues, discuss new resources, and exchange ideas on how to effectively market library resources. Policies and resources are captured in a LibGuide so that it can be referred back to in the future. This process of learning together, sharing thoughts on how to tackle challenges, and experimenting with tools empowers the LMU librarians to improve outreach to their departments, as well as strengthens the trust they have in the library's collections decisions.

STORYTELLING

A communications concept that can assist librarians when conveying information about their collections is that of storytelling. Libraries have always existed to tell stories to the reader: from preschoolers to faculty, for popular and scholarly audiences, and through fiction and nonfiction. Traditionally, however, the library itself has not been the focus of the story. The need to create a story about ourselves was never in great demand because we have benefited from the wellspring of positive feelings people have customarily associated with libraries, often taking the form of platitudes about how "the library is the heart of the university" in higher education.

As the role of libraries has changed, we face the downside of that latent good will. Notions of what libraries are and should be are often "suspended in amber": nostalgia for a time that never was and certainly is not today's reality (Seeber 2018). In the face of this traditionalism and wistfulness, librarians are now tasked with the need to explain what libraries are becoming. These conversations can be even more difficult to have when antiquated ideas are held by our strongest supporters. Libraries need to be able to tell hard truths about the challenges we face in order to fully support the educational mission of our institutions. While context is important for the positive stories of our successes, it is imperative when discussing bad news, whether a deselection project, journal cancellations, or simply saying "no" to a resource request. A broader story about how these decisions are made is required in order to achieve campus buy-in and support.

Why is storytelling important? Humans are wired for stories—we want to tell them and we want to hear them: "Stories explain, inspire, comfort, and in general help us understand the complexities of daily life in small and large ways" (Marek 2011, 4). The increasing emphasis on marketing and outreach as essential functions of contemporary libraries has led to a greater understanding of the need to tell libraries' stories. "A compelling story that illustrates the impact of a program or service on a real person will always be more interesting than a list of facts or a collection of descriptive statements" because stories provide "a framework for understanding all of our outreach and communication efforts" (Mansfield 2016, 40–41). Storytelling as a communication method has been explored for libraries in general (Marek 2011) and for reference librarians specifically (Colón-Aguirre 2015). Collection development libraries have their own challenging array of topics to address, including the marketing of electronic resources (Kennedy and LaGuardia 2018), deselection of materials (Held 2018), and journal cancellation mandates (Hardy, Zimmerman, and Hanscom 2016); however, the use of storytelling techniques has not been widely discussed in the collection development literature.

There are communication and storytelling principles that collections librarians can apply to strengthen their messaging. The first is knowing the intended audience and customizing the message for that audience. "Know when to go for a hard sell, and know when to just have a conversation over a cup of coffee. Know when pie charts and spreadsheets are called for, and when a story about impact on a student is a better choice" (Rogers and Wesley 2015, 73). Recognizing the differing levels of baseline knowledge between faculty and our librarian colleagues, as well as the political consequences of topics that may be noncontroversial with an internal audience and hotly contested with an external campus audience (e.g., deselection of print materials), will also influence the methods and word choices we use. A related and aforementioned principle is providing clear, concise, and consistent messaging. This is particularly important when collection librarians formulate messages that are delivered by liaison libraries with differing levels of knowledge about the topic.

A second factor to consider is the use, and sometimes abuse, of data as a storytelling tool. We are by now accustomed to the need to make the case for our services, our spaces, and our collections. We have a long history of using data to support our claims, from the first time a librarian ever tracked how often scrolls were consulted through the growth of evidence-based librarianship of recent decades (Eldredge 2000). The challenge is using data to support the story while knowing that data is not the story itself. Data is necessary, but not sufficient. While faculty respect data, the higher education literature is full of examples of the limits of unemotional, rational, data-driven deselection projects that hit the immovable wall of faculty opposition. As Dellinger notes, "To effectively persuade others, you need *proof* that speaks to both the head and the heart" (2009, 85). And that, in a nutshell, is storytelling.

Real-World Examples of Storytelling

Sometimes storytelling is for an audience within the library. An example from LMU is the "Electronic Resources Usage Statistics Dashboard" (LMU).

While this site is useful to library administrators, the primary audience has been the liaison librarians. Librarians want information about electronic resource usage, and there is certainly a tidal wave of data available. However, just providing a number is of limited value, without context and benchmarks against which to make comparisons. Marie Kennedy, serials & electronic resources librarian, and Marisa Ramirez, electronic resources assistant at the time, created the dashboard to respond to liaison requests for information (Kennedy and Ramirez 2015). The dashboard shows aggregate use by publisher or vendor, but also "top 10" lists and quick facts about the type of resource. The dashboard format is flexible enough that a new type of resource, such as streaming media, can be added by including another tab. A high-level overview of the data is presented annually at an all-librarians meeting. The dashboard has proven to be a popular way to provide liaisons with an understandable snapshot of electronic resource use, but was never intended to answer all usage questions at all levels of granularity. Since its rollout, commercially available services have entered the marketplace, such as RedLink Library Dashboard, but no matter what tool is used, the goals for LMU are still the same: to help liaisons understand the library's own e-resource story, to empower the librarians to be able to do their jobs better, and to shape the narrative for the wider institutional community.

A second example, this time of external storytelling, comes from the UCSF Library, where the scholarly communications and collection development librarians created a webpage on the library's website to tell the story of the serials crisis to their users and to explain how this ongoing industry issue has affected the library's ability to subscribe to new resources. This page was created as a way to better respond to the many questions that have been received regarding why the library does not have a subscription to certain, much-needed journals and why the library often cannot afford to subscribe at the time they are requested. In addition to including a link to this page during many of our patron exchanges, it is also added to publicity during our annual subscription review process when we ask for feedback on proposed cancellations so that our patrons can be better informed as to why the library needs to look at cutting lower-used resources.

The "Journals Cost How Much?" page uses appropriate language for this external audience, limiting its use of "library speak" and is careful to not overwhelm the reader with too much information (UCSF Library). Data visualization best practices were also applied to the page's graphs. The graphs are not cluttered, only show the most pertinent information, and support the story that is being told regarding the rapidly increasing cost of journals. For more information regarding best practices for data visualizations, the white-paper section of Tableau's website provides great documentation (Tableau), as do books like *Data Visualization: A Guide to Visual Storytelling for Libraries* (Magnuson 2016) and *Effective Data Visualization: The Right Chart for the Right Data* (Evergreen 2016). Also found on the UCSF page are links to additional resources about the serials crisis, so readers can dive deeper into the topic if their interest has been sparked, and next steps for ways concerned community members can get involved in the campuswide scholarly communication efforts.

COMMUNICATION STRATEGY ASSESSMENT

Assessment has been a very popular topic for librarian publications and presentations over the past few years. Borne out of a need to continually demonstrate our value to directors, provosts, chancellors, and others in order to reassure them that they are making a good investment in funding their campus libraries, assessment can provide the hard numbers and statistics that, along with anecdotal or qualitative evidence, can complete the library's intended story. Just as collection development librarians keep track of and assess numbers like circulation statistics, usage statistics, cost per use, and pricing changes, they should also be keeping track of and assessing their communication efforts. Assessing our communication strategies enables us to know if we are effectively reaching our users and provides us with the data to identify trends over time.

As with any assessment project, knowing your end goal will guide you through developing a strategy for assessing communication. Before the communication strategy assessment can take place for a particular communication event, the strategy should ideally tie to a larger marketing plan that, in turn, should be tied to the library's strategic plan. The literature on library marketing emphasizes the importance of not only having a marketing plan in place but also including assessment as part of that plan: Lucas-Alfieri recommends asking, "How did the team gather data and how and when do they plan to reassess the progress they have made through their market planning and promotional efforts?" (2015, 37) and Duke and Tucker suggest that "a concerted effort should be made to measure the effectiveness of the marketing activity" (2007, 58). In the absence of a library marketing plan, the communication strategy should at least support the larger library goals. Once the communication strategy is in alignment with the larger library vision, the three-step process of marketing analytics outlined by Jerry Rackley can be applied. In the chapter, "The Marketing Analytics Process," in his book, *Marketing Analytics Roadmap*, he explains that the three steps are identifying metrics, analyzing metrics, and taking improvement actions (2015).

The objectives outlined in the larger communication plan or library strategic plan should serve as the basis for identifying which marketing metrics you will be assessing. The metrics you track during the communication event must be able to measure the progress toward these objectives (Rackley 2015). Depending on the type of objectives that are being pursued, metrics may include "users' awareness level; customer satisfaction; participation; number of users; [and] usage of resources, services, programs" (Duke and Tucker 2007, 58). Once the proper metrics are selected, analysis begins by capturing and keeping track of them. "The goal of this analysis step is to draw insights from the data about marketing's progress toward achieving its objectives" (Rackley 2015, 51). For electronic communications, there are many systems and tools that make capturing these metrics very easy, if not automatic. Instead of e-mailing a campus distribution list or listserv directly through your e-mail client, utilize an e-mail marketing platform like MailChimp or Constant Contact. These platforms track open rates, click rates, repeated views, and more, so you can easily determine if your message is being viewed and how widely you are reaching your users. Similarly, hosting files on a cloud server like Box and linking to the file in the cloud on a webpage or in an e-mail instead of uploading it directly to the website server or attaching it to an e-mail will also allow for click rates to be tracked.

Once the current state of metrics is captured, it must be compared with what the ideal outcome is in order to identify how effective the communication event was. "Knowing whether any particular measurement result is good, bad, or indifferent requires some sort of comparison, to historical data or a set of benchmarks that represent a standard of excellence" (Rackley 2015, 52). If this comparison does not meet expectations, or even if it does and you wish to replicate the success, you will need to determine which changes will most likely lead to or maintain the ideal outcome. There is no magic bullet, and different messages often require different methods or repeated efforts to reach your target audience. It can be especially tricky when your ideal viewers or responders do not fall neatly into a specific school, department, or staff designation. Extra effort will need to be made in order to reach these elusive users so that a balanced and fair cross-section of opinions is reflected in your results. Conducting market research and tests, such as A/B testing, can help determine which improvements to make. While time intensive and, at times, less prescriptive than other parts of assessment, these actions can be well worth the effort "because it helps ensure that improvement actions are the right ones the first time. . . . The causes of ideal outcomes form the basis of best practices that help the organization consistently achieve the desired results" (Rackley 2015, 55–56).

A willingness to change direction if the method you have utilized is not providing you with the results you are hoping for is essential to marketing success. "As a matter of fact, a marketing plan that does not develop and change over time means that it is not being used. In this case, an always changing plan is a good thing" (Duke and Tucker 2007, 63). Additionally, communication strategy assessment is most effective when the process is repeated continuously. "Repetition of the analytics process is necessary to produce consistent and sustained improvement. . . . Remaining vigilant to the analytics process is the way to ensure the best long-term performance of marketing" (Rackley 2015, 56).

Real-World Examples of Communication Strategy Assessment
The UCSF Library conducts an annual journal subscription review to identify lesser-used titles that could be cancelled in order to realize cost savings. A list of these candidates is posted to the library website, as well as announced to the campus via an e-mail distribution list, and feedback is requested from our users to ensure that they play a role in the cancellation process. In the past, a dedicated e-mail was sent directly from the collection development librarian to the campus, and the list of proposed cancellations was uploaded

directly to the website server. In 2015, the library started to utilize Box to host files that are linked to on the website, and this change enabled us to view the access statistics for these files. Also in 2015, the library hired a communications manager who shifted our e-mail marketing from e-mailing the campus directly from our e-mail client to sending e-mails through the MailChimp platform, which, again, provided us with all sorts of metrics to use to evaluate our effectiveness.

In 2017, in an effort to reduce the number of e-mails sent to the entire campus, the communications manager included the journal cancellation announcement and call for feedback in the monthly library newsletter instead of sending a dedicated e-mail like in years past. After a week, the list of cancellations was only viewed 12 times, and no comments were received. Years of past data informed us that these statistics were unusually low, and the communications manager then sent a dedicated reminder e-mail to the campus distribution list. The views jumped up to over 700 once this e-mail was sent out, and the collection development librarian received the anticipated number of comments. If the UCSF Library had not been able to view how many times the list had been accessed and then compare it to past data, we would not have been able to determine as easily why we were not receiving as many comments as usual. We were able to change direction with our communication and send the reminder as a dedicated e-mail, seeing the effectiveness immediately in the large jump of document views. Due in large part to this strategy, the UCSF Library was ultimately able to cut 16 journals titles in 2017 with very little pushback.

At the UVA Library, the collections team regularly confronts the challenge of gathering information on resource needs and then assessing and prioritizing expensive resource requests from faculty, students, administrators, and subject liaisons across all disciplines and departments. Purchase recommendations for expensive resources are often focused on individual research or teaching interests, generally proffered in isolation from other requests being made from across the institution, and usually advanced through the collections process via subject liaisons. Recognizing that a single access point, an individual subject liaison, might not be sufficient as the primary means of gathering information from many researchers on needed resources, the collections team launched web-based request forms by resource type (e.g., data sets, journal article databases, primary source documents) to improve this communication process.

Data from the various forms is collected in a central location that then can be accessed by any library staff member. Because the internal notes, decisions, and timelines for each requested resource are collected in a single, convenient location, this information is immediately available to subject liaisons to be shared with requesters and other interested users. To gain a holistic view of campus needs, the collections team also looks for commonalities and anomalies gleaned from purchases and interlibrary loan requests, as well as from notes taken from conversations with users, librarians, and vendors. Using simple text analysis, this information is then used to augment the resource-decision matrix as well as spark collections conversations among disparate subject domains to enhance the understanding of resource needs.

As a result of the new request forms deployment, the collections team has seen an increased number of purchase suggestions across all disciplines from all levels of scholars. Having access to all of the resource recommendations in one place provides the team with unfiltered information and the opportunity to see where holistic and interdisciplinary needs exist across the institution. By providing an additional channel for users to request purchases, researchers no longer have to be filtered through their subject liaisons and instead can have direct contact with the collections team members for increased engagement around resource acquisition.

CONCLUSION

Collections librarians should never underestimate the importance of good communication with their internal and external stakeholders. "You have to start gathering your resources now, creating your networks, establishing frameworks, building your relationships in context, and demonstrating your expertise, so that when you reach your point of need, you have as much as possible available to support you" (Rogers and Wesley 2015, 71). The success of a major change could come down to how effectively you were able to communicate with your users and colleagues. Finding a seat at an existing table in your community or creating the missing table yourself will enable collections issues to be more visible and to shift the idea that decisions are only made within the library to one where users have a voice in what happens. Consistent and transparent communication with library colleagues will enable collections librarians to create trustful advocates who can assist in spreading messages and receiving feedback.

The communication methods we employ have a significant impact on how our message is received. Acknowledging the human responsiveness to storytelling by adjusting the language for your audience and not relying on data alone could cause an increase in the receptiveness of your users to the library's cause. Lastly, just like any other data we collect, librarians should constantly be assessing our communication efforts to keep track of effectiveness. We must be willing to remain agile and change our method if our desired outcomes are not being reached. Communication about collections should not only occur when a potentially negative change is taking place; it should be a regular part of every collection development librarians' responsibilities.

BIBLIOGRAPHY

ACRL. "2016 Top Trends in Academic Libraries." *College & Research Libraries News* 77, no. 6 (2016): 274–281.

ALA. "ALA's Core Competences of Librarianship." Accessed June 10, 2018. http://www.ala.org/educationcareers/sites/ala.org.educationcareers/files/content/careers/corecomp/corecompetences/finalcorecompstat09.pdf.

ALCTS. "Core Competencies for Acquisitions Professionals." Accessed June 10, 2018. https://alair.ala.org/handle/11213/9058.

Camack, Angela. "Playing Triple—A Ball with Faculty: How to Use Advocacy, Access, and Authority in Liaison Activities." Accessed July 2, 2018. http://www.choice360.org/blog/playing-triple-a-ball-with-faculty-advocacy-access-and-authority-in-liaison-activities.

Colón-Aguirre, Mónica. "Organizational Storytelling Among Academic Reference Librarians." *Portal: Libraries and the Academy* 15, no. 2 (2015): 233–250.

Dellinger, L. K. L. "A Values-Based Approach to Successful Library Advocacy." In *The Library PR Handbook*, edited by Gould, Mark, 81–94. Chicago: American Library Association, 2009.

Duke, Lynda M. and Toni Tucker. "How to Develop a Marketing Plan for an Academic Library." *Technical Services Quarterly* 25, no. 1 (October 18, 2007): 51–68. doi:10.1300/J124v25n01_05. http://www.tandfonline.com/doi/abs/10.1300/J124v25n01_05.

Eldredge, Jonathan D. "Evidence-Based Librarianship: An Overview." *Bulletin of the Medical Library Association* 88, no. 4 (2000): 289.

Evergreen, Stephanie D. H. *Effective Data Visualization: The Right Chart for the Right Data.* Sage Publications: Thousand Oaks, CA, 2016.

Fisher, William. "Core Competencies for the Acquisitions Librarian." *Library Collections, Acquisitions and Technical Services* 25, no. 2 (2001): 179–190. doi:10.1016/

S1464–9055(01)00190–7. http://www.sciencedirect.com/science/article/pii/S146490 5501001907.

Hardy, Beatriz Betancourt, Martha C. Zimmerman, and Laura A. Hanscom. "Cutting without Cursing: A Successful Cancellation Project." *The Serials Librarian* 71, no. 2 (August 17, 2016): 112–120. doi:10.1080/0361526X.2016.1196635. https://doi.org/10.1080/036 1526X.2016.1196635.

Held, Tim. "Curating, Not Weeding." *Technical Services Quarterly* 35, no. 2 (2018): 133–143.

Hurley, Robert F. "The Decision to Trust." *Harvard Business Review* 84, no. 9 (2006): 55–62.

Johnson, Peggy. *Fundamentals of Collection Development and Management.* 4th ed. Chicago: ALA Editions, 2018.

Jones, Melissa. "Being Earnest with Collections: Improving Internal Communications at Georgetown University." *Against the Grain* 29, no. 1 (2017): 70–75. https://against-the-grain.com/2017/03/v29-1-being-earnest-with-collections/.

Kennedy, Marie R. and Cheryl LaGuardia. *Marketing Your Library's Electronic Resources: A How-to-Do-It Manual for Librarians.* 2nd ed. Chicago: American Library Association, 2018.

Kennedy, Marie R. and Ramirez, Marisa, "Visualizing Electronic Resources Data Using a Statistics Dashboard" (2015). *LMU Librarian Publications & Presentations.* 21. http://digitalcommons.lmu.edu/librarian_pubs/21.

Lucas-Alfieri, Debra. "Creating the Marketing Plan." In *Marketing the 21st Century Library*, edited by Lucas-Alfieri, Debra, 31–39: Waltham, MA: Chandos Publishing, 2015. http://www.sciencedirect.com/science/article/pii/B9781843347736000040.

Magnuson, Lauren. *Data Visualization: A Guide to Visual Storytelling for Libraries.* Lanham, MD: Rowman & Littlefield, 2016.

Mansfield, Clarissa J. "The Role of Stories in Library Marketing and Communications." *OLA Quarterly* 21, no. 4 (2016): 39–45.

Marek, Kate. *Organizational Storytelling for Librarians: Using Stories for Effective Leadership.* Chicago, IL: American Library Association, 2011.

NASIG. "NASIG Core Competencies for Electronic Resources Librarians." Accessed June 10, 2018. https://amo_hub_content.s3.amazonaws.com/Association92/files/CoreComp/Compe tenciesforERLibrarians_final_ver_2016-01-26.pdf.

Rackley, Jerry. "The Marketing Analytics Process." In *Marketing Analytics Roadmap*, 45–56. Berkeley, CA: Apress, 2015. https://link.springer.com/chapter/10.1007/978-1-4842-0259-3_4.

Rogers, Jenica P. and Kathryn Wesley. "Reaching New Horizons: Gathering the Resources Librarians Need to Make Hard Decisions." *The Serials Librarian* 68, no. 1–4 (May 19, 2015): 64–77. doi:10.1080/0361526X.2015.1016831. http://www.tandfonline.com/doi/abs/10.1080/0361526X.2015.1016831.

Seeber, Kevin. "Amber." Accessed July 2, 2018. http://kevinseeber.com/blog/amber.

Tableau. "Tableau Whitepapers." Accessed July 2, 2018. http://www.tableau.com/learn/white papers.

Trenholm, Sarah and Arthur Jensen. *Interpersonal Communication.* 6th ed. New York: Oxford University Press, 2008.

Turner, Lynn H. and Richard West. "Theories of Relational Communication." In *Making Connections: Readings in Relational Communication*, edited by Galvin, Kathleen M. and Pamela J. Cooper, 20–34. Los Angeles: Roxbury Publishing, 2006.

UCSF Library. "Journals Cost How Much?" Accessed July 2, 2018. http://www.library.ucsf.edu/open-access/journals-costs/.

THE PAST IS PROLOGUE: TELLING OUR STORIES ABOUT TEXTBOOK AFFORDABILITY PROGRAMS

Jeanne Hoover
Scholarly Communication Librarian, Research and Scholarly Communication, East Carolina University, hooverj@ecu.edu

Cynthia Shirkey
Head of Collection Development, East Carolina University, shirkeyc@ecu

ABSTRACT

Textbook prices have increased exponentially in recent years. To combat this problem, East Carolina University has initiated two textbook affordability programs to help reduce textbooks costs for students. In this chapter, the authors share information about these programs as well as tips to start similar services.

INTRODUCTION

The cost of college tuition has continued to rise in recent years. Along with that, the cost of textbooks has seen a huge increase. According to the Bureau of Labor Statistics, Consumer Price Index for textbooks rose by 88%, while college tuition and fees rose by 63% between 2006 and 2016.[1] With costs rising, students are looking to reduce their costs, at least when it comes to textbooks. In 2016, Florida Virtual Campus surveyed students on textbooks and course materials. According to the results, 66.6% of students did not

---

1. Bureau of Labor Statistics, U.S. Department of Labor. "College Tuition and Fees Increase 63 Percent since January 2006." *The Economics Daily*. Accessed May 22, 2018. http://www.bls.gov/opub/ted/2016/college-tuition-and-fees-increase-63-percent-since-january-2006.htm.

purchase a required textbook due to cost.[2] Students also took fewer classes, chose other courses, or dropped a course due to textbook costs.[3] However, the most concerning data stated that 37.6% of students earned a poor grade and 19.8% of students failed a course due to textbook costs.[4] It is evident that the cost of textbooks may be inhibiting students to be successful in college.

In response to textbook costs, a movement toward textbook affordability initiatives has started to pop up in universities and, most notably, in libraries, across the country. The details of these initiatives vary and range from circulating current textbooks to purchasing unlimited user e-books to providing stipends for faculty to use open educational resources (OER). Libraries have also collected textbooks to lend to students to help with textbook costs. The texts typically have a shorter checkout time to allow a greater number of students to use them.

More libraries are getting involved with textbook affordability initiatives like unlimited user e-books or faculty stipend programs aimed at including OER. E-book textbook programs allow all students to access the materials thanks to availability of unlimited user licenses. These programs tend to be in the library, while open textbook initiatives may be housed in other departments on campus. While there are multiple definitions of OER, they generally incorporate the following: a variety of materials that are free for end users that include a public domain or Creative Commons license that allows for adapting and remixing.[5,6] OER can include a wide range of materials such as textbooks, videos, tests, syllabi, and lectures. Lately, there has been an increase in state legislatures acknowledging and funding programs to help reduce the costs of textbooks for university students. The most

2. Florida Virtual Campus. "2016 Florida Student Textbook & Course Materials Survey." Accessed May 22, 2018. https://florida.theorangegrove.org/og/items/3a65c507-2510-42d7-814c-ffdefd394b6c/1/.
3. Ibid.
4. Ibid.
5. United Nations Educational, Scientific, and Cultural Organization. "What Are Open Educational Resources (OERs)?" Accessed May 22, 2018. http://www.unesco.org/new/en/communication-and-information/access-to-knowledge/open-educational-resources/what-are-open-educational-resources-oers/.
6. William and Flora Hewlett Foundation. "Open Educational Resources." Accessed May 22, 2018. http://www.hewlett.org/strategy/open-educational-resources/.

THE PAST IS PROLOGUE 39

recent data shows that 24 states either have or are considering a law that includes mandates for addressing concerns around textbooks.[7] Examples of established statewide programs include Open Oregon and Affordable Learning Georgia.

At East Carolina University (ECU), there are two textbook initiatives that, while separate, complement each other. Textbooks may be purchased as an unlimited user e-book, or faculty may receive a stipend to switch out their current textbook to include OER or library materials.

East Carolina University, or ECU as it is known in the region, is a school of about 29,000 FTE, including online students. Approximately 22,000 attend on-campus classes, and the remaining 7,000 are distance education students. ECU is a Carnegie classification doctoral universities: Higher Research Activity school with 4 professional doctoral degrees, 13 research doctoral degrees, and a medical and dental school. There is a main campus and a west, health sciences campus, but both function as one campus online. Geographically it is about an hour and a half east of Raleigh and about an hour to an hour and a half west of the Outer Banks. It is a part of the 17-school University of North Carolina (UNC) system, being the fourth largest in the system. Students matriculate to ECU from all over the state, making ECU a racially and economically diverse university. There is also a small out-of-state population and a small international cohort.

The history of ECU's textbook affordability programs goes back to 2015, when Patrick Carr, who was, at the time, assistant director for Acquisitions & Collection Management for ECU, oversaw the course-adopted textbook program.[8] He had come back from a ULAC (University Libraries Advisory Committee—a group comprised of library deans and directors from the 17 UNC system schools) gathering and had heard a talk about how UNC-Charlotte was doing a textbook affordability program that focused

7. SPARC. "OER State Policy Tracker." Accessed May 22, 2018. https://sparcopen.org/our-work/state-policy-tracking/.

8. Patrick L. Carr, James D. Cardin, and Daniel L. Shouse. "Aligning Collections with Student Needs: East Carolina University's Project to Acquire and Promote Online Access to Course-Adopted Texts." *Serials Review*, 42, no. 1 (January 2016): 1–2, https://doi.org/10.1080/00987913.2015.1128381.

on course-adopted texts gathered from the bookstore. He was inspired and immediately saw that ECU could emulate Charlotte's program. The first step was getting the list of course-adopted texts from the book store. This proved to be challenging, but after getting support from the Provost, the book store became a willing partner and has remained so. Next, Carr developed a workflow for dealing with the book store data. The spreadsheet sent to us by the book store is very large; it contains a line for everything ordered for a class for a particular term. The spreadsheet first gets cleaned: all the non-book items, the course-packs, and the items with access codes get sifted out because the library can't supply them. Then, the resulting spreadsheet gets checked in Gobi (ProQuest's Yankee Book Peddler's book vending system) to see what we have access to and what we can purchase in an unlimited license format and for how much.

The unlimited license format is key. Although there have been times, for smaller classes, we've gone with other types of licenses, unlimited license format provides the best utility for this program. It is the only way to know for sure that all students in the class will always have access to the text. It is the most expensive license for e-books, but when you break it down on a cost-per-use basis, it is an expense well worth it.

After we know the universe of what we could purchase, we make collection development decisions about what we will purchase. Generally, we consider factors like book cost and class size when deciding what to purchase—we try to do the most good for our money. We purchase what we've chosen and then enter it into a spreadsheet.

The spreadsheet is very important because it's how we record our success with the program. The spreadsheet has columns for author, title, year of publication, print ISBN, e-ISBN, instructor, course code, section, number of students enrolled, bookstore price, Gobi price, and proxied URL. Most of the fields are self-explanatory; however, bookstore price is a bit of a head-scratcher. Many book stores have two prices listed: new and used. We always go with new if possible. It is important to decide which one you will use because book store price is used to calculate maximum potential savings, a concept we will talk more about later in this chapter.

Also in that spreadsheet goes the data for any unlimited license course-adopted texts we may have already owned. Once that spreadsheet is complete, it gets uploaded into a database so that faculty and students can search for their texts and find links to them. Our database can be found at https://lib. ecu.edu/alt-texts. The final step is to send an e-mail out to all faculty teachers with these texts so they can in turn let their students know about the availability of the free e-books.

In 2016, Joseph Thomas, Cindy Shirkey, and Beth Bernhardt wrote an LSTA grant for the state of North Carolina to expand this program. Thomas (assistant director for Collections and Scholarly Communication) and Shirkey (head of Collection Development) work at ECU, while Bernhardt (assistant dean for Collection Management and Scholarly Communications) works at the University of North Carolina at Greensboro. ECU was interested in sharing its know-how for the course-adopted textbook program with UNCG, while UNCG had successfully piloted an alternative textbook mini-grants program the year before that ECU was interested in learning from UNCG. The grant, which covered fiscal years 2017 and 2018, was awarded for both campuses to do both halves of the alternative textbook programs. In the end, these authors were awarded $161,065 for both campuses, for both years.

The alternative textbook mini-grants program, as run by ECU's Jeanne Hoover (scholarly communication librarian), is simple: it pays professors to revamp their courses using OER or no-cost (to students) library resources. In the spring of each year, you can have informational meetings where you talk about the program: your expectations, what the deliverable would be, what the compensation will be, and so on. Try to reach as many faculty members as possible. Have an application process where each faculty member submits a syllabus and a form that explains how he or she wants to update the syllabus to use free resources. You can create a rubric to score the applications that considers factors like cost of current textbook, student enrollment, learning outcomes, and a detailed plan on incorporating new materials into the curriculum. You should assemble a group of respected faculty and librarians to score the applications and make the awards. Our awards have been for different amounts, but $1,000 is a good round number. This is money that gets paid directly to the faculty members, so they can use it as they see fit. Payment should be made during the summer, which is when the bulk of the work will be done, as well.

One word about payment: research disbursement thoroughly at your institution before initiating this program. At ECU, we found it was a lot more difficult to achieve than we thought it would be. One unfortunate fact that surfaced was that, due to the way the money is paid out, fixed-term faculty cannot receive it. Because fixed-term faculty do not have continuing contracts, they are not eligible for payment during the summer. If this is the case at your institution, it is better to be up front about it from the beginning.

The next step of the mini-grants is to pair winners with personal librarians. It helps if the librarian has personal knowledge of the subject the faculty member is teaching, but that is not required. It is more important that the librarian be willing to learn about OER and Creative Commons licensing attributes, to tell which items in the catalog have unlimited licenses and have a can-do attitude. The personal librarian-faculty relationship is very important because faculty have an idea of what they'd like to do by this point in the mini-grants program; they just need help executing it.

The time commitment it takes for each personal librarian to help his or her faculty member varies. Some faculty already have a clear idea of where to go and how to get there. Others need much more help. It's not uncommon for the whole project to take more than 40 hours of a librarian's time, just as it's not uncommon for it to take less than 10 over the course of an academic year.

It is also not uncommon for the two programs to merge in practice. A mini-grants winner may very well find that the perfect text substitution is one that can be purchased in an unlimited license format via the course-adopted textbook program. The students do not care how they get free texts, and if we have the money to fund purchases, neither should we.

How do we measure success in either course-adopted texts or alternative textbook mini-grants? There are a variety of ways. With course-adopted texts, we can look at number of faculty reached, number of courses impacted, number of students impacted, books purchased and cost savings, return on investment, and maximum potential savings. Maximum potential savings is figured by taking the book store cost and multiplying it by the number of students registered for the course. This is the maximum number we could be saving each term. At ECU we have found that we usually see a maximum potential savings of around $200,000 or more each term. That's with spending approximately $5,000 per term on course-adopted texts. For spring term 2018, our return on investment was $26.18 for every dollar spent. To date, we have saved students a maximum potential savings of over $1 million. We have worked with hundreds of faculty, thousands of students, and over 1,200 classes.

With alternative textbook mini-grants we can measure number of faculty participating and number of syllabi revised. But really, it comes down to the quality of the experience with the new materials in the newly revamped syllabus and that is hard to measure objectively. To date at ECU we have had 45 faculty participate, including the current cohort, and 28 syllabi revised.

While the programs at ECU have been relatively successful, there are items to consider when starting a textbook affordability program. Not all the textbooks that faculty needed were available as unlimited user e-books. While this is to be expected, we ran into circumstances where a text was available, but it was an older edition. This can cause issues, especially if the edition used in the classroom is not clear when the library purchases titles. We also found that some faculty were not interested in participating in the program because they received author royalties from books they had written and chose to use in their classroom. However, the library purchased the title and made it available for students on the free e-textbook website. The direct link to the book is not listed in the course's course management site. Finally, we found some titles that we believed we had access to through a package, but the book only allowed for a limited amount of views. When these titles were discovered, we removed them from the free e-textbook database and our spreadsheet.

Most of issues that we ran into with the mini-grant program came from paying the stipends to faculty. Like many universities, we have tenured tenure-track faculty and fixed-term faculty. We had issues making payments to fixed-term faculty for various reasons, including contract or grant funding restrictions. Faculty who applied to the mini-grant gave an overview of resources they could use to replace their textbooks. Unfortunately, there are not enough resources, especially open resources, to cover some of these classes. In these circumstances, we relied heavily on unlimited user e-books. This was also difficult due to the guidelines of the program and restrictions of our funding. Our program asked faculty to replace all their texts in the course with materials that were free for students. However, for some topics, it may have been a better approach to have flexibility with keeping a low-cost text for class, especially if the topic was not represented in OER or unlimited user e-books.

For the past two years, our course-adopted textbooks and mini-grant programs have been funded through a large grant. Our future initiatives will be changing as we are taking on the cost of the programs again. The course-adopted program will be absorbed in our materials budget. While the available funds will not be as high, we will still be able to purchase new texts for faculty and students. Our current catalog of e-textbooks is extensive, and we hope that faculty will use those texts and editions for a few years.

The mini-grant program will be more difficult to continue due to costs. However, it may be possible to review the program and potentially reduce the number of stipends offered per year. This could open the opportunity to accept more complex projects and to be more involved than in the past. As mentioned earlier, the payments made to faculty can be difficult for various reasons, including type of faculty contract and cancellation of classes. We will be reviewing payment options to see if there is a more streamlined approach. For example, making payments only to the department, applying the stipends after completing the program, or requiring funds to be used for a graduate assistant support are all possibilities. In our first year of the program, we provided stipends only for faculty teaching during the fall semester. Classes may change or be cancelled based on student registration. This can cause an issue for faculty who are funded for later semesters. Funding per semester or year will be reviewed again for the next round of applications.

The textbook affordability programs are impacting our campus and saving students money. Many faculty who have participated in either program are looking to incorporate more free or low-cost texts in their other classes. We hope to continue this shift and see more students saving money while also getting more customized texts for their courses.

A TALE OF TWO TEXTBOOK PROGRAMS: SEEKING A SUSTAINABLE MODEL FOR TEXTBOOK ACCESS IN ACADEMIC LIBRARIES

Serin Anderson
Collections & Budget Coordinator, University of Washington
Tacoma Library, serin@uw.edu

Suzan Parker
Head, Collections and Course Support Services,
Anthropology Librarian, University of Washington
Bothell & Cascadia College, sparkerz@uw.edu

ABSTRACT

Academic libraries have long wrestled with how to address the common question, "Does the library have my textbook?" With textbook affordability conversations accelerating across campuses, many academic libraries have become actively engaged in exploring ways to help students and faculty manage the challenge of rising textbook prices. The following case study details how two branch campus libraries at the University of Washington Bothell and Tacoma campuses initially approached textbook course reserves when they started in 1990, and the arc of changes that both applied in the search for a sustainable textbook program.

INTRODUCTION

Conversations about textbook affordability and open educational resources are gaining traction and visibility across the nation with advocacy by student groups and state legislators. A recent NBCNews.com article reports that "textbook prices have risen over three times the rate of inflation from January 1977 to June 2015, a 1,041 percent increase."[1] A consequence of this increase is that many students have inadequate or no access to required course materials. One e-textbook industry-sponsored research study reported that "85% of students had delayed or avoided altogether purchasing textbooks for their courses, with 91 percent of these students citing cost as the reason. Half of the students said that their grades had been negatively impacted by their decision."[2] And possibly affecting time-to-graduation, a frequently cited 2014 Public Interest Research Group report stated that "nearly half of all students surveyed said that the cost of textbooks impacted how many/which classes they took each semester."[3]

Clearly textbook prices are having negative financial and academic impacts on many of our students. But how exactly can or should the library respond to student and faculty requests to purchase textbooks? From the library perspective, they're expensive, are rapidly outdated, and take up increasingly valuable shelf space. From the student perspective, having a textbook available through the library may reduce financial burdens and contribute toward their academic success.

TWO UNIVERSITY OF WASHINGTON CAMPUSES, TWO APPROACHES

Founded as upper division degree completion programs in 1990, the founding missions of the University of Washington Bothell[4] and the University of Washington Tacoma[5] were to serve time-bound/place-bound students, particularly returning adult and transfer students completing four-year degrees. UW Bothell and UW Tacoma both started as 2+2 models, i.e. students started their first two years at another community or four-year college, followed by two years of courses at the upper division to complete their bachelor's degree

1. Popken, Ben. "College Textbook Prices Have Risen 1,041 Percent since 1977," *NBC News* online, last modified August 6, 2015, http://www.nbcnews.com/FEATURE/FRESHMAN-YEAR/COLLEGE-TEXTBOOKPRICES-HAVE-RISEN-812-PERCENT-1978-N399926
2. McKenzie, Lindsay. "Study: High Textbook Prices Lead to Poor Grades," *Inside Higher Ed* online, last modified September 20, 2017, http://www.insidehighered.com/quicktakes/2017/09/20/study-high-textbook-prices-lead-poor-grades
3. Senack, Ethan. "Fixing the Broken Textbook Market," *U.S. PIRG: The Federation of State PIRGS*, last modified January 27, 2014, https://uspirg.org/REPORTS/USP/FIXING-BROKEN-TEXTBOOK-MARKET
4. "Bothell from the Beginning," *University of Washington Bothell*, accessed July 29, 2018, http://www.uwb.edu/about/history
5. Wadland, Justin and Charles Williams. "University of Washington Tacoma," HistoryLink. org online, last modified November 7, 2017, http://historylink.org/File/20469

in liberal studies (now known as interdisciplinary arts and sciences). In 2006 both campuses began offering lower division courses and expanded their curricular offerings, particularly in STEM fields. After a 2011 Higher Education Coordinating Board report[6] documented increased employer demands for baccalaureate graduates, both campuses responded with a comprehensive range of undergraduate, master's, and professional programs. Since that 2011 report, UW Bothell (5,669 FTE)[7] and UW Tacoma (4,763 FTE)[8] have boosted the number of students by 40–50% and continue to make significant contributions to serving the educational needs of their regions.

As part of the "one library, three campus" model of the University of Washington Libraries, the UW Bothell and UW Tacoma Libraries have developed their print and electronic collections with a local, interdisciplinary curricular focus, while relying on the comprehensive collections of the UW Seattle campus and Orbis Cascade Alliance consortial partners to provide more extensive research-level resources. This has enabled both campus libraries to focus on building interdisciplinary collections that meet the needs of an increasingly diverse student population, represented by significant numbers of nontraditional students, students of color, immigrants, first-generation college students, veterans, and international students.

From the beginning, the UW Bothell and UW Tacoma Libraries have taken fundamentally different approaches to the question of textbooks purchased by the library. The UW Bothell Library cultivated a robust textbook course reserve program with proactive purchase of nearly every assigned book, including traditional textbooks, while the UW Tacoma Library opted for a more typical approach by restricting the purchase of most textbooks. Over the years, the UW Bothell Library has modified its textbook program, as needed. More recently, after an alarming spike in costs, a textbook task force was convened to conduct a thorough data review. As a result, the UW Bothell Library is now focusing resources on higher-use/higher-cost items. Taking the UW Bothell Library task force findings into consideration, the UW Tacoma Library is now adopting

---

6. "Regional Needs Analysis Report," *Washington Higher Education Coordinating Board*, last modified March 2011, http://www.wsac.wa.gov/sites/default/files/RegNeedsAnalysis-Binder.pdf

7. "Fast Facts 2017–2018," *University of Washington Bothell,* accessed July 30, 2018, http://www.uwb.edu/about/facts/fast-facts-2017

8. "Student FTE by Class Level and Program 2017–18 Autumn," *University of Washington Tacoma Institutional Research Reports.*

a more open approach with a nascent textbook program first piloted in early 2017. Both libraries agree that equity and access are a primary consideration for their textbook programs. However, long-term sustainability for their collection budgets is also a concern. Taking the long view, each library is exploring ways to partner with faculty and other campus partners to bring down student textbook costs by expanding awareness of open educational resources (OER) and other affordable alternatives to high-cost, traditional textbooks.

UW BOTHELL: CASE STUDY OF A TEXTBOOK PROGRAM AT 25+ YEARS

Located on 128 acres in a suburban neighborhood north of Seattle, UW Bothell overlooks a 58-acre wetland restoration project. The branch campus is co-located with Cascadia College,[9] a community college, and serves a two-county region north and east of Seattle. From the beginning, the UW Bothell Library initiated a policy to purchase and place on reserve *all* required course texts. This was over 25 years ago, when UW Bothell offered classes only at the upper division, primarily in liberal studies. At that time, the liberal studies program did not typically use traditional textbooks, so it made sense to purchase all required texts under the assumption that these books would likely have been purchased for the general collection anyway. It should be noted that our textbook purchasing program was never intended to take the place of students buying copies of their books. It was intended to build our interdisciplinary collection, from scratch initially, and had the added benefit of being convenient for our commuter students. At the time, this was a good collection development strategy for building an interdisciplinary, curricula-focused collection.

Until recently, UW Bothell experienced the fastest growth rate of any public university in Washington State. As the number of majors and classes offered at UW Bothell grew, so did the need for more collections funding and staff time devoted to course reserves. With the addition of lower division courses and growth in STEM degree programs, the number of traditional textbooks used in introductory and survey courses also increased, resulting in even higher costs for course reserves. And while the UW Bothell campus has quickly grown to almost 5,700 FTE, the library's available collections budget

---

9. Since 2000, UW Bothell has shared a co-located campus with Cascadia College. Textbooks are not purchased for Cascadia courses but are placed on reserve if already owned by the UW Libraries. This case study focuses on textbook acquisitions for UW Bothell classes only.

has not increased at the same rate. Additionally, like academic libraries everywhere, the UW Bothell Library is experiencing significant pressure on the collections budget due cost inflation for serials and databases.

As the campus has grown, the library has periodically reassessed textbook purchasing policies and made some adjustments over time. Exceptions that have been added to the general policy include the following:

- Beginning in 2009, most business textbooks were excluded from purchase due to their cost and budgetary impact. This change provided funding for additional databases and other electronic resources that support undergraduate and graduate business degrees.
- Due to a pattern of low (or no) circulation, physical items are not placed on reserve for off-site programs in nursing and business since these students would need to travel long distances to use them.
- Reserves staff request approval from librarian selectors before purchasing textbooks over $200. Most higher-cost textbooks are ultimately purchased, but occasionally selectors solicit faculty input and opt to use previous recent editions. Library staff also encourage faculty to place personal or donated copies of texts on reserve.

With these caveats, our reserves unit staff generally purchased or placed on reserve all other required textbooks for UW Bothell classes until fall quarter 2017. Changes to our textbook purchasing program resulted from a data-driven analysis conducted in 2016–2017, by UW Bothell Library staff.

UW BOTHELL: IMPLEMENTING A TEXTBOOK TASK FORCE

As it was becoming increasingly evident that our 25+-year-old textbook purchasing model was becoming unsustainable without significant changes, the director of the UW Bothell Library brought together a textbook task force in 2016 to consider options. Task force members included our library director, head of Collections, head of Access Services, and Reserves supervisor.[10] Task force members were committed to continuing to provide a robust textbook

---

10. The authors wish to acknowledge the contributions of UW Bothell Library staff, librarians, and former colleagues toward this analysis, especially Kayla Johnson, Sarah Leadley, Jennifer Patterson, and Mary Yutani.

program at the Bothell campus. However, we wanted to make a data-informed decision about how collections and staffing resources were being allocated and why. We hoped that patterns emerging from the data would help guide us in our recommendations for policy changes. Our data points included a scan of textbook practices in other academic libraries, textbook circulation data, historical spending patterns and other costs, and UW Bothell student responses from UW Libraries' Triennial Survey.

The task force started by reviewing information compiled in 2014 about textbook purchasing policies from over 120 academic institutions[11] across the United States, as well as 13 University of Washington libraries. At the time the data was gathered, a large majority of libraries did not automatically purchase all or most textbooks. Of those libraries that did have some type of textbook purchasing program, most did not have significant funds available or dedicated to this. Libraries with textbook programs also typically required faculty to make a formal request first. Some libraries had additional criteria related to high-enrollment classes, course level, or expensive textbooks. This environmental scan confirmed that Bothell's practice of automatically purchasing nearly every required textbook was uncommon among academic libraries.

Textbook Circulation Data Analysis

The task force members, based on anecdotal evidence as well as from frontline public service experience, assumed that students were using reserve textbooks more than items in the general collection, and that they checked out the highest-cost items the most. Task force members checked these assumptions by analyzing reserves circulation and cost data of new textbook purchases from summer quarter 2015 through spring quarter 2016. Surprisingly, *overall* usage of new textbooks on reserve turned out to be lower than expected.

Total circulation of newly purchased reserve textbooks, summer 2015–spring 2016:

- 695 checkouts for 354 items
- Average circulation per item = approximately two checkouts
- 69% of these books had zero or only one check-out

---

11. "Reserve Textbook Policies by Institution," *University of Washington Bothell Library,* accessed July 25, 2018, https://tinyurl.com/y72bgmaf

As a point of comparison, the *average for circulated items* for the UW Bothell Library general collection as a whole for the 2015–2016 academic year was *0.75* (this includes both initial circulation and renewals but does not include materials that had zero circulation). The average for *all* items in the general collection (including those that were not used at all) was calculated at just *0.22* in 2017–2018. Thus, while reserve textbooks did not have especially high usage overall, they were used at a significantly higher rate than books in the general collection.

The task force then analyzed the average circulation (Table 1) and average cost per use (Table 2) and discovered that the most circulated items fell into the middle and high ranges of cost. This was not particularly surprising since we assumed financially burdened students would be more likely to borrow the most expensive books.

The task force also looked for patterns of usage by course level and found that textbooks on reserve were used most often for courses at the 200-level, followed by the 300-level. Items at the 200-level also happened to have the highest average cost. However, their cost per use was also the lowest since these expensive books circulated more frequently.

There were no discernible patterns of use by subject matter, and in some cases, we found textbooks were used frequently for one quarter, but not the next. And while we could see which books were being used, and for which classes, the available data could not answer the most pertinent questions about our users: *Which students were relying on these textbooks? How often? And Why?* In order to protect borrower privacy, UW Libraries' circulation data does not account for unique borrowers. Circulation data does not report whether there are multiple students checking out a specific reserve item, or a smaller number of students checking out items repeatedly.

TABLE 1. Average circulation, newly purchased reserve items by cost, summer 2015–spring 2016

Cost	Total new spent	# New items	# New checkouts	Average circulation/new item
$1–$49	$5,227	223	287	1.18
$50–$99	$3,025	42	103	2.45
$100–$199	$6,632	43	202	4.70
$200+	$4,708	19	77	4.05
Total	**$19,592**	**327**	**669**	**1.96**

TABLE 2. Cost and usage by course level, summer 2015–spring 2016

Course level	Total #	Total spent	Average cost	Average circulation	Average cost per use
100	59	$3,005.92	$50.95	1.89	$26.96
200	44	$2,929.87	$66.59	3.27	$20.36
Lower division (combined 100/200 level)	**103**	**$5,935.79**	**$57.63**	**2.5**	**$23.05**
300	79	$4,950.01	$62.66	2.51	$24.96
400	86	$5,222.76	$60.73	1.63	$37.26I
Upper division (combined 300/400 level)	**165**	**$10,172.77**	**$61.65**	**2.05**	**$30.07**
Master's (500 level)	58	$3,255.79	$56.13	1.62	$34.65

Cost Considerations

Fortunately for our students, and for our collections budget, we discovered that the average cost of about $60 for a UW Bothell class textbook turned out to be quite a bit lower than the average price of $80 for a new textbook, as reported in 2015–2016 by the National Association of College Stores.[12] However, the 36% spike in reserves spending in the 2013–2015 spending cycle was alarming and signaled the need to redirect collections resources to support our textbook purchasing program or to consider a more sustainable model.

An analysis of historical reserves spending patterns over 10 years showed an increase of 45% from 2007 to 2017 (Table 3). This increase was attributed to various factors, including textbook inflation, program growth, and more frequent adoption of traditional textbooks for lower division survey courses (e.g., introduction to biology or introduction to psychology). This spending increase came even after business courses were excluded from Bothell's textbook purchasing program in 2009 (prior to that, business textbooks represented 24% of all reserve monograph purchases).

Another cost consideration was the staffing resources needed to provide the service. At the time of the program review, UW Bothell Library reserves staff estimated that they were spending an average of four to six hours per day during peak busy weeks of the quarter and two to four hours per day during nonpeak weeks of the quarter on tasks related to reserves textbooks, including

12. "Higher Education Retail Market Facts & Figures: Textbook Prices," *National Association of College Stores*, accessed July 22, 2016, http://www.nacs.org/research/HigherEdRetailMarket FactsFigures.aspx

TABLE 3. Trends in monograph reserves spending at UW Bothell

2005–2007	2007–2009	2009–2011	2011–2013	2013–2015	2015–2017	% increase: 2007–2017
$29,617	$30,669	$27,474[a]	$30,380	$41,434	$42,801	44.51%

[a]Business textbooks were excluded from the purchase program in 2009.

UW Bothell undergrad survey responses: importance of course reserves

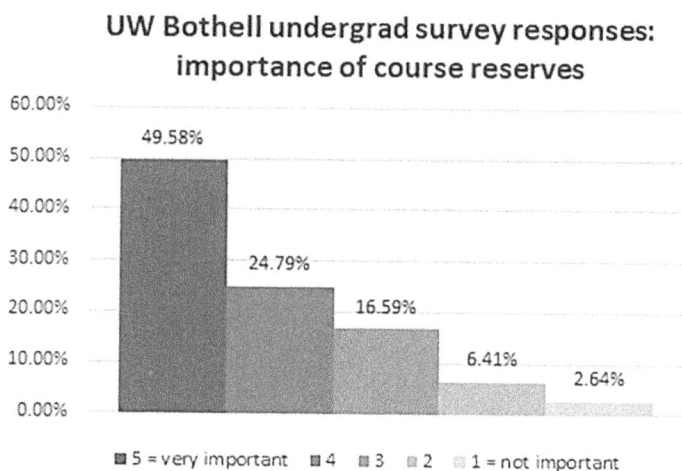

- 5 = very important
- 4
- 3
- 2
- 1 = not important

49.58% 24.79% 16.59% 6.41% 2.64%

FIGURE 1. UW Bothell undergraduate responses to a question on the 2016 Triennial Survey

ordering, processing, and tracking. The total average number of hours spent per quarter was approximately 250 hours. Time spent during the summer quarter was minimal and was not included in these estimates. These staffing time estimates also did not include cataloging or other overhead costs.

Student Stakeholders

We know from the most recent UW Libraries 2016 Triennial Survey[13] data that having textbooks on reserve is important to those students who are aware of the service and use it. In the 2016 survey, three-quarters of UW Bothell undergraduate students responded to the question, *how important are course reserves (e.g., textbooks, films) to your work?* with a rating of 4 or 5, on a Likert scale of 1 (low) to 5 (high). Half of undergraduate students rated the importance of course reserves as 5, or "very important (Figure 1)."

---

13. "2016 Triennial Survey," *University of Washington Libraries*, accessed July 24, 2018, "http://www.lib.washington.edu/assessment/surveys/triennial." Please see the 2016 Bothell Undergrad Survey Form.

Selected student comments from the survey echo these findings. Students across class levels expressed appreciation for the service, noting that having textbooks on reserve helped lower their expenses, enabled them to leave heavy textbooks at home, and provided a critical option to completing assignments when textbook orders hadn't yet arrived at the bookstore. However, students also expressed dissatisfaction: they wanted *more* copies of textbooks to be available, longer checkout periods, more online textbook options, and increased representation of textbooks in their subject areas:

> More reserve textbooks, one or two is not enough (First Year)
>
> Have all textbooks that are required for classes accessible as reserves, but an online PDF would be best (Sophomore)
>
> If students can borrow textbook for the whole quarter, that will be great. (Junior)
>
> The reserves greatly help me get my text book cost down. (Junior)
>
> At the beginnings of quarters before my textbooks arrive library staff is very helpful in helping me find and borrow their copies so I can do my homework. (Junior)
>
> [Being able to check out the textbook overnight] was helpful since my text book I ordered had not arrived yet. (Junior)
>
> Course reserves are also helpful because we can't always carry out huge books around so it's nice to be able to check out the book to study while on campus (Junior)
>
> The library course reserves have helped me a lot for my classes. I can't afford the books so having a textbook I can checkout is VERY helpful. (Senior)
>
> Reserve books should be given for more than 2 days. (Graduate)
>
> I strongly [recommend] to provide [the] online course book. I know so many students [are] happy to save money. Course books are expensive. (Graduate)

UW BOTHELL: RECOMMENDATIONS FOR POLICY CHANGES

As our task force researched the issue, it became clear that UW Bothell Library's textbook reserve program was unique in the UW Libraries (and among academic libraries across the country). Task force members grappled with options and did not take lightly the impact that changes might have on students. Options under consideration were as follows:

A. *Continue current practice:* automatically purchase nearly all UW Bothell textbooks for reserves. Consult with librarian selectors on whether to purchase titles over $200.
B. *Limit textbook purchases to those over a certain price point* (e.g., $100+ or $200+).
C. *Use a phased approach:* make incremental changes to current practices over time (i.e., purchase over a certain price point for a fixed duration, then discontinue practice of automatically purchasing required textbooks).
D. *Discontinue practice of automatically purchasing required UW Bothell textbooks* for reserves as of a certain date (e.g., next academic year).

After soliciting input from staff across the UW Bothell Library, and in consideration of circulation, cost data, and student survey feedback, the task force recommended *Option B*. Recognizing that "affordability" is relative, we proposed making a first small step by changing the policy to exclude automatically purchasing books under $50.

UW Bothell Library, Updated Textbook Purchasing Policy (effective fall quarter, 2017):

• Reserves staff will discontinue automatic purchase of textbooks under $50. Titles not purchased for reserve will be forwarded to selectors and/or the head of Collections to be considered for purchase for the general collection.
• Reserves staff will continue to automatically purchase textbooks over $50 and continue to purchase textbooks exceeding $200 with selector approval.
• Circulating copies of textbooks already owned by UW Libraries will be placed on reserve without regard for the price point.

Rationale

The task force noted that the average circulation of new materials under $50 was comparatively low—only 1.18 circulations on average (Table 4). We also

TABLE 4. Average circulation for newly purchased reserve items by cost, summer 2015–spring 2016

Cost	Total new spent	# New items	# New checkouts	Average circulation/new item
$1–$49	$5,227	223	287	1.18
$50–$99	$3,025	42	103	2.45
$100–$199	$6,632	43	202	4.70
$200+	$4,708	19	77	4.05
Total	**$19,592**	**327**	**669**	**1.96**

noticed that two-thirds of new textbook purchases for reserves fell under $50, a cost level that we had determined was relatively "affordable" for our students. We speculated that low circulation of lower-cost items indicated that students were more likely to purchase these materials or were able to find copies through other means than course reserves. This change would hopefully have a minimal negative impact on students, and it would significantly decrease the number of books that we were ordering for reserves, many of which were duplicated in the system elsewhere.

UW BOTHELL: IMPACT OF CHANGES AFTER ONE YEAR

An immediate and noticeable impact of this change is that Bothell's *spending on reserve textbooks dropped by about half.* This was a much bigger savings than anticipated. From 2013 to 2017, the UW Bothell Library spent an average of $21,059 per year. After implementing these changes, reserves staff spent $10,694 on textbooks during fiscal year 2017–2018. In addition to the $10,694 spent for textbooks on reserves funds, selectors and the head of Collections opted to spend another $1,061 from general collection funds for course texts that were under the $50 limit, for a revised total of $11,755 (Table 5). This represents a *44.18% decrease* from the previous four years' average.

This cost reduction only accounts for differences in collections spending. It does not factor in staff time to request and process additional transfers between locations. However, additional staff time spent on processing transfers is mitigated by time not spent on ordering, cataloging, and marking new items. The impact of these changes on staff workload is anecdotal observation and has not been formally calculated.

TABLE 5. Cost and circulation comparison of newly purchased and previously purchased reserve items, summer 2017–spring 2018

Cost	Total new spent	# New items	# New checkouts	Average circulation/ new item	# All items	# All checkouts	Average circulation/all items
$1–$49	$770	37	23	0.62	698	824	1.18
$50–$99	$2,524	33	120	3.64	150	449	2.99
$100–$199	$4,105	27	106	3.93	183	1,013	5.54
$200+	$4,356	16	26	1.63	143	645	4.51
Total	**$11,755ª**	**113**	**275**	**2.43**	**1,174**	**2,931**	**2.50**

ªIncludes an additional $1,061 from general collections funds for course texts that were under the $50 limit.

In examining the circulation data for 2017–2018, we can see that the $100–199 range circulates most frequently, which is consistent with the 2015–2016 data. What seems counterintuitive is that there is a noticeable drop-off in circulation at the $200+ level for both new and previously purchased reserve items. We attribute this decrease in average circulation to the fact that these books are in closed reserves (i.e., behind the desk) and not as accessible to our users. Additionally, some of these texts are for specialized courses of study, such as mechanical engineering, and may not have large numbers of students taking those courses.

Adjustments to the New Policy

We amended our new policy after just two quarters when we discovered that there were a disproportionate number of required texts for our interdisciplinary arts, creative writing, literature, and cultural studies courses that were under $50, but not owned by any other UW Library. It was an unintended consequence that students in these programs were put at a disadvantage just because their course texts tend to be less expensive. Students in these courses are often required to purchase several different texts for one class, which can quickly meet or exceed the cost of a regular textbook. When we realized the change to our textbook purchasing policy was impacting students in these disciplines, we quickly changed the policy to include purchasing anything under $50 that was not duplicated elsewhere in the system. With the relatively minimal extra cost of $1,061, we were able to support students in these programs in a more equitable manner, while enhancing UW Libraries' collections by adding these unique titles to the system.

UW TACOMA: CASE STUDY OF A TEXTBOOK PROGRAM IN DEVELOPMENT

While similar in many ways to UW Bothell—beginning as an upper division, access-oriented institution with a curricularly driven collection—the local organizational culture and practices produced a Tacoma collection development environment that typically eschewed the purchase of traditional textbooks. For many years, assigned texts not defined as "textbooks" were actively purchased and added to the collection but were not automatically placed on reserve. Selectors added traditional textbooks only on an ad hoc basis, and reserves were routinely based on faculty requests alone. However, a series of changes across campus triggered a self-assessment and exploration of different models.

In 2016, the Tacoma campus rolled out a new strategic plan built with wide input from campus stakeholders and the surrounding community.[14] In many respects, the plan built on a campus identity shaped by membership in the Coalition of Urban Serving Universities where the vision for students states: "Urban universities put me first; it reflects the diversity of my city, levels the playing field so that everyone thrives, and its purposeful engagement in the city prepares me for the changing worlds of career and community life."[15] Highlighting a number of impact goals and success indicators focused on student success and equity, the new strategic plan reflected not only general trends in higher education but also the reality of an institution serving a community of students where approximately half identify as a minority, over 93% are in-state residents, and almost 60% of first-year students come from families where parents do not have college degrees.[16]

By the fall of 2016, as the new campus strategic plan kicked into high gear, a series of events spurred conversations and questions about providing access to textbooks. A July 2016 piece published on *The Atlantic* website, titled "When College Students Need Food Pantries More Than Textbooks,"

---

14. "Charting Our Course: UW Tacoma's Strategic Plan 2016–2021," *University of Washington Tacoma*, accessed July 20, 2018, http://www.tacoma.uw.edu/sites/default/files/sections/Chancellor/ChartingOurCourse-2018.pdf
15. "Mission & Vision," *Coalition of Urban Serving Universities*, accessed July 19, 2018, http://usucoalition.org/about/mission
16. "Quick Stats of Student Enrollment," *University of Washington*, accessed July 15, 2018, https://studentdata.washington.edu/quick-stats/

highlighted a new report pointing to growing demands for emergency aid programs.[17] The article was shared on the campus website (noting a quote from a former campus administrator). Meanwhile, a local faculty member continued to share research about Tacoma students experiencing food insecurity, with the student newspaper highlighting her work in an article about the food pantry on campus.[18] Soon after, staff reviewing data from the UW Libraries' 2016 Triennial Survey observed comments from Tacoma graduate students specifically calling for textbook access similar to the long-running UW Bothell Library program, despite the fact that none of the Tacoma surveys included a question asking about the importance of course reserves:[19]

> I regularly check out required textbooks through UW Bothell's library (UW Tacoma's library has none) and interlibrary loan. This has saved me THOU-SANDS of dollars in required textbook purchases that I didn't have to make over the course of my [degree] program.
>
> . . . In my opinion, UW Tacoma library should have a copy of ALL REQUIRED TEXTBOOKS available for CHECKOUT—NOT REFER-ENCE! for each and every class offered on campus. Students regularly have to pay $200 to $300 for a book they may use a handful of times, often just to look up assigned homework questions. There is no need to purchase these, this is something the library should provide. UW Bothell's library does, why doesn't UW Tacoma's???

Additionally, library staff attending new student orientations in fall quarter 2016 reported a noticeable uptick in questions about the availability of textbooks. While certainly not unusual, many UW Tacoma students transfer from local community colleges, and two of the top transfer schools include Tacoma Community College and Pierce College: schools active in statewide initiatives to develop infrastructure and materials for OER and programs to

---

17. Deruy, Emily. "When College Students Need Food Pantries More Than Textbooks," *The Atlantic* online, last modified July 9, 2016. http://www.theatlantic.com/education/archive/2016/07/when-college-students-need-food-pantries-more-than-textbooks/490607/
18. "UW Tacoma Homelessness a Serious Issue," *The Tacoma Ledger* online, last modified February 2, 2017, http://thetacomaledger.com/2017/02/06/uw-tacoma-homelessness-serious-issue/
19. "2016 Triennial Survey."

reduce the impact of purchasing traditional textbooks. Within a matter of weeks, internal staff meetings throughout winter quarter 2017 resulted in a proposal for a textbook pilot beginning in late March 2017.

UW TACOMA: SPRING 2017 PILOT

The initial pilot design hinged on selecting programs that would provide a representative snapshot of materials and student use, but would also allow the pilot team to target communications with discrete, self-contained academic programs. Given substantial unknowns about staff capacity to sustain a textbook program in the long term, the team felt that targeted communications would reduce the risk of setting expectations campus-wide. With those parameters in place, the team selected the Institute of Technology and the Urban Studies program for a single quarter pilot. Both programs included a mix of undergraduate and graduate degrees, while the assigned texts ranged from highly technical traditional textbooks to an interdisciplinary mix of textbooks and nonfiction. With the exception of an all-faculty e-mail, the communication strategy focused on sending information about the pilot directly through program staff, so that all messages would be disseminated by the departments to program-specific listservs. Concurrent e-mails were drafted and sent to each program's faculty and student lists prioritizing information on checkout and availability, location of the physical reserves, and the overarching goal for the pilot: to provide data that would help the library staff determine if it was possible to create an ongoing, sustainable program to support textbook access for those *most in need* (which we did not define). The expectation was not that the library would be able to provide all textbooks for every class, but to hopefully create a structure that would allow library staff as well as the faculty and students to help identify where we could best target our funding and time.

The goals for the spring pilot program also encompassed understanding the scope of changes needed to update or alter workflows and procedures and, perhaps more importantly, required estimating the capacity of existing staff to support additional work, including:

- *Establishing a workflow for retrieving textbook data.* The local bookstore manager was a supportive partner in the pilot; however, the data was typically shared in a printout that required manually entering each title into a spreadsheet. Reserves staff then conducted one to two manual searches of all relevant curriculum codes on the University Bookstore website to identify late faculty textbook submissions.

- *Making key format decisions.* The texts purchased for the pilot were primarily print books, although e-books available with appropriate licensing, unlimited users, and no DRM were included and linked to course reserves when available. If textbooks came with codes or similar single-use electronic access, the material was removed from the title during processing.

- *Creating an ordering workflow and revising reserve procedures.* Ordering procedures were drafted for both print and electronic material, and staff received training. Additionally, base circulation parameters were set—four-hour checkout with no holds—for texts purchased or added to course reserves as part of the program. In the normal procedures, faculty stipulated course reserve terms (often two-hour, four-hour, one-day, or three-day checkouts) when they initiated a reserve request.

- *Creating new reserve usage reports.* Prior to the textbook pilot, a reserves usage list was run only on a quarterly basis. Beginning spring quarter 2017, a new weekly reserves report was created and pushed out via e-mail to staff. Rather than capturing all material on reserve, the weekly report provided a list of all titles used, including the date and time of checkout. With each week's data appended to a single spreadsheet, the data offered the potential to view title use patterns for particular titles or courses throughout the quarter.

At the conclusion of the spring 2017 pilot, there were a variety of questions about use of the texts and perceptions of faculty and students from the two target programs. Short online surveys were sent to program faculty and staff at the end of quarter. Given the timing and limited communication about the program, a very small set of responses were received—26 student surveys and 4 faculty surveys, but they did provide a view into some of the issues the program faced. Although multiple e-mails were sent through the departmental representatives, half of the student respondents said they were unaware of the textbook pilot. Unsurprisingly, given that half were unaware, 18 students indicated that they had not used any of the textbooks; however, when asked if an expanded textbook program would be a valuable service for campus, 18 students or 70% said they strongly agreed, 5 students or 19% said they somewhat agreed, and 3 students or 12% indicated that they were neutral. When asked to share thoughts or comments, most highlighted a known or perceived need.

> I think it is a great idea for people who are struggling to afford college. Some of my classmates did not use textbooks during entire quarters at all.
> I have friends who struggle to buy, rent, or borrow books and if this program was expanded it would help them a lot.
> As a student who uses VA, all my books are covered through VA at no cost to me. I have many non-veteran classmates that would simply NOT buy the textbook at all for a class due to the high cost. The proposed textbook pilot would an incredible benefit for those students.

Similarly, the four faculty respondents, two from the Institute of Technology and two from the Urban Studies program, were all supportive of the pilot program, and all indicated that they strongly agreed with an expanded pilot being valuable for campus. While survey feedback was overall positive, use of the spring 2017 pilot textbooks closely mirrored trends in Bothell with only 40% of the titles circulating.

UW TACOMA: 2017-2018 EXPANDED PILOT

The local textbook team, despite a somewhat limited dataset, recommended moving forward with an expanded pilot that offered the opportunity for a deeper examination of why and when students might opt for limited-use, library-provided textbooks. The expanded program incorporated a series of parameters based partly on the experience of the spring 2017 pilot but also on the data collected in UW Bothell Library's 2016 textbook program review.

Early stages of the data analysis concentrated on evaluating the potential volume of items that staff might need to process. Using the fall 2016 title list provided by the University Bookstore, the team estimated total number of volumes and a rough estimate of cost for a single quarter based on four

TABLE 6. Scenario comparisons based on University Bookstore data for fall 2016

Scenarios with price cutoff	Rough cost estimate	Number of titles
One copy of every title	$39,000	537
Titles > $50	$32,000	252
Titles > $75	$28,000	187
Titles > $100	$24,000	140

scenarios (Table 6). To some surprise, the estimated number of course reserve titles dropped by almost 60% if purchased textbooks only included those $75 and over, and cost estimates dropped by approximately 18–38% when compared with the scenario of purchasing one copy of every title.

Concerns about workload capacity and questions around the availability of reserve shelving space meant that the total number of items to be processed was given considerable weight, but two additional factors influenced the final parameters. Early conversations with the local University Bookstore manager centered on bookstore staff observations of student behavior. According to the manager, students were often more hesitant about buying textbooks over $100, frequently looking for textbook rentals, e-books, or other less expensive options. Early on, the team found this information useful, but not entirely actionable. It seemed anecdotal until data from the Bothell program review demonstrated that reserve items at or over that same $100 price point had more than twice the average circulation per item. With that information in hand, final decisions for the expanded pilot included:

- Purchasing course texts for all schools, departments, or programs with a new purchase price of $75 and over.
- Encouraging both students and faculty to request purchase of titles falling under the $75 price point via a web form.
- Purchasing a second copy of texts only when there were four or more sections of courses using the same text.
- E-books were added to reserves (as a stand-alone) only if they were unlimited use with limited or no DRM.

Beyond the program parameters, the major push for the expanded pilot centered on communication strategies and experimentation with different methods of capturing data not visible in regular circulation numbers. Given the significant e-mail communication barriers that surfaced in the spring 2017 pilot survey data, the new communication plan largely centered on website changes and direct student outreach. Prior to the start of fall 2017 quarter, a new "button" was added to a prominent position of the library's main home page with all-caps text, "DOES THE LIBRARY HAVE YOUR TEXTBOOK?" The result page provided an overview of the pilot, a course reserve search box, and a short FAQ with contacts.[20] A brief article written by a graduate student library employee also described the program in a news format that was then linked from a set rotation of "Library Stories."[21] Additionally, all in-person orientations with new students included information on the expanded pilot.

UW TACOMA: EARLY ASSESSMENT AND CURRENT STATE

The data now being collected is less about making explicit decisions than about identifying information that can help us discover meaningful patterns, refine data collection, and develop effective tools for evaluating use over time. For example, during the spring 2017 pilot, there was an attempt to capture turn-away data by adding a note when recording a desk question in Springshare's LibInsights product (Figure 2). However, without some kind of visible reminder, it was difficult for student employees or regular staff to remember to add the note. Later discussions with the UW Libraries' director of Assessment and Planning led to a new "Reserve textbook turn-aways" radial button that allowed anyone at a service desk to quickly indicate that a textbook had been requested but was either checked out or not on reserve. Adding a note about which course it was for was an option, but not required. While discussions about making this change occurred in the summer and fall of 2017, it wasn't implemented until winter quarter 2018. However, even once the radial

---

20. "University of Washington Tacoma Library," *Wayback Machine Internet Archive* online (website capture), last modified October 24, 2017, https://web.archive.org/web/20171024193009/www.tacoma.uw.edu/textbook-support
21. Wigren, Erika. "Borrow Textbooks for Free from the Library," *University of Washington Tacoma Library*, last modified November 6, 2017, http://www.tacoma.uw.edu/library/article/borrow-textbooks-free-library

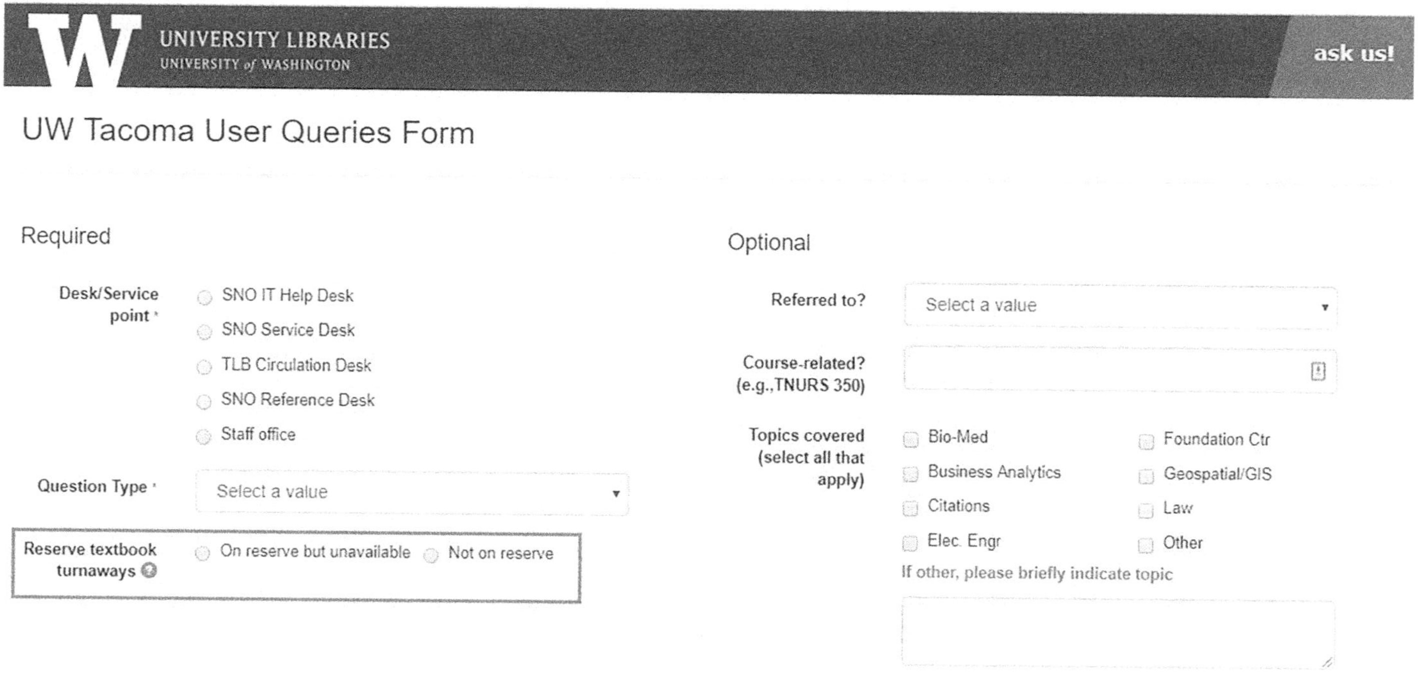

UNIVERSITY LIBRARIES
UNIVERSITY of WASHINGTON

ask us!

UW Tacoma User Queries Form

Required

Desk/Service point *
○ SNO IT Help Desk
○ SNO Service Desk
○ TLB Circulation Desk
○ SNO Reference Desk
○ Staff office

Question Type *   Select a value ▸

Reserve textbook turnaways ⊕
○ On reserve but unavailable   ○ Not on reserve

Optional

Referred to?   Select a value ▸

Course-related? (e.g., TNURS 350)   ⊞

Topics covered (select all that apply)
☐ Bio-Med   ☐ Foundation Ctr
☐ Business Analytics ☐ Geospatial/GIS
☐ Citations   ☐ Law
☐ Elec. Engr   ☐ Other
If other, please briefly indicate topic

FIGURE 2. Screenshot of Springshare's LibInsights desk tracking form used at UW Tacoma Library

TABLE 7. Use of a textbook, *Starting out with Python*, over a four quarter period

Spring 2017 Initial pilot			*Fall 2017*			*Winter 2018*			*Spring 2018*		
April	May	June	October	November	December	January	February	March	April	May	June
4	2	0	4	1	2	1	1	0	10	8	1
6 total uses			7 total uses			2 total uses			19 total uses		
3 course sections			3 course sections			2 course sections			2 course sections		
83 students total			85 students total			70 students total			59 students total		

button was active, only 53 uses were recorded during winter and spring 2018 quarters with an almost 50/50 split between "not on reserve" and "on reserve but unavailable." It's not clear if the small reported number is because there were fewer turn-aways than expected or rather due to a training gap.

The circulation data, while seemingly straightforward, presented both stumbling blocks and intriguing questions. For example, a title on reserve for the same class over four different quarters demonstrated an increase in use in spring 2018 (Table 7). Such a trend could raise questions about potential differences in the number of sections, students, or perhaps different faculty. Yet, the data appears counterintuitive with spring 2018 showing higher use, fewer students, and the same faculty. While there is no definitive answer for this single course, one possible factor could boil down to different communication. During the second week of spring quarter 2018, the campus newspaper published an article titled "UWT Library Continues to Provide Expensive Textbooks to Students."[22] After reviewing the weekly reserve statistics, there was a sudden increase in use right after the article was published, with use tapering off the remainder of the quarter. With a relatively limited data set, the team hasn't drawn any conclusions but now plans to document major outreach events to evaluate if it is possible to identify high-impact outreach methods.

Unfortunately, we also realized that the weekly reserve statistics had supplanted a previous quarterly report that captured all reserve titles regardless

---

22. Wood, Robbie. "UWT Library Continues to Provide Expensive Textbooks to Students," *The Tacoma Ledger* online, last modified April 2, 2018, http://thetacomaledger.com/2018/04/02/uwt-library-continues-provide-expensive-textbooks-students/

of use. Because of the current procedures for creating course reserves in Ex Libris' Alma Analytics, it was impossible to go back and re-create the reports after the fact. Beginning fall quarter 2018, major circulation data captures will include:

- Quarterly report of all reserve titles with circulation totals.
- Weekly report of all reserve titles used.
- Textbook turn-away data captured through desk statistics.

At the conclusion of the 2017–2018 academic year, estimates for the number of titles and total cost, largely based on fall quarter 2016 University Bookstore data, fell within acceptable ranges, and the reception of the program on campus was overwhelmingly positive (Table 8).

Moving forward, for the 2018–2019 academic year the textbook program will continue with the same parameters with one exception: we will not be proactively purchasing a second copy of any course texts unless we are able to identify significant turn-aways at the course level. During the expanded pilot, only a small number of titles met the criteria for two copies (four or more concurrent sections or courses using the same text), and usage data did not indicate that the second copies were in high demand. A more in-depth evaluation of the program is planned after the second full year of data to include a wider survey, focus groups, and an analysis of outreach methods.

TABLE 8. Comparison of estimates to actual number of titles processed and cost for 2017–2018

	Estimate for fall 2017	Estimate for 2017–2018 (based on 25–50% over fall)	Actual totals for 2017–2018
Total number of titles purchased	187	234–281	322
Total cost	$28,000	$35,000–42,000	$42,983
Number of titles purchased under $75 price point	x	x	63
Cost of titles under $75 price point	x	x	$2953

[a] The totals are for FY18 in full, not limited to the fall, winter, and spring academic quarters.
[b] For values labeled as unknown, there was no attempt to estimate number of titles or cost.

CONCLUSION

As responsible stewards of our limited resources, academic librarians must balance varying user needs as we allocate funding toward services and collections. In grappling with whether to purchase textbooks, we must consider how the general collection might be impacted, and whether we are still able to meet the curricular and research needs of our students and faculty. Purchasing high-cost, traditional textbooks that frequently change editions can decrease purchasing power to build these general collections. In addition to hitting our collections budgets, providing textbooks can be a labor-intensive process for library staff. It might seem on the surface that library-purchased textbooks are a luxury that the library can't afford. At the same time, many of our students struggle to meet even basic needs. Too often, they are faced with difficult choices between necessities such as food, childcare, healthcare, and housing; or covering their educational costs, including skyrocketing tuition and textbooks.

At the UW Bothell and UW Tacoma Libraries, we recognize that many of our own students face these economic challenges, especially as the cost of textbooks has risen dramatically in the past decade. Our respective textbook programs are an attempt to provide some measure of relief to our students. However, we acknowledge that our current practices are supplementary at best and do not ultimately fix the problem of high textbook costs. Providing one or two copies of a textbook on reserve may not serve students at their point of need, particularly on commuter campuses serving significant numbers of nontraditional students who can't always flex their schedules to be available when their textbook is.

So how do we develop a sustainable model for textbook programs? For now, the answer may lie in finding a middle ground of textbook support that the budget can sustain for a period of time while the market continues to evolve. At the same time, we can partner with campus stakeholders to more widely adopt alternatives to traditional textbooks, such as open, affordable, and licensed educational resources (OER, AER, LER).

In our case study examples, scaling back an "all-in" model allowed UW Bothell Library to minimize unnecessary print duplication across the tri-campus UW Libraries system, and to redirect collection resources toward under-funded and high-demand formats such as streaming video and unlimited use e-books. Establishing a nascent textbook program at UW Tacoma Library initiated an emerging dialog with the campus community about the benefits and limitations of library-provided textbooks. Meanwhile, local OER teams[23] and cross-campus initiatives[24] continue to explore how to support faculty to identify or create high-quality open educational resources, consider affordable educational resources (generally those $50 or less), and integrate existing licensed educational resources provided through the library. As both campuses look to the future, this multipronged strategy continues to evolve with sustainability as a core value.

---

23. OER LibGuide from the University of Washington Bothell Library, http://guides.lib. uw.edu/bothell/open
24. A list of OER-related work and cross campus initiatives at the University of Washington Libraries, https://guides.lib.uw.edu/c.php?g=417242&p=2843433

REIMAGINING RESEARCH SERVICES AS PART OF MAJOR ACADEMIC LIBRARY RENOVATIONS OR OTHER CHANGES: A TALE OF TWO RESEARCH DEPARTMENTS (UNIVERSITY OF CENTRAL FLORIDA AND FLORIDA GULF COAST UNIVERSITY)

Barbara G. Tierney
Head of Research & Information Services, University of Central Florida Libraries, Barbara.Tierney@ucf.edu

Linda K. Colding
Head of Reference, Research, & Instruction, Florida Gulf Coast University Library, lcolding@FGCU.edu

ABSTRACT

Two academic library research service managers discuss changes and innovations that they have coordinated in their respective libraries (University of Central Florida serving 60,000+ students http://library.ucf.edu/21st/[1] and Florida Gulf Coast University serving 15,000+ students http://library.fgcu.edu/admin/renewal.html[2]) due to major building renovations or other changes that their respective libraries are conducting.

---

1. University of Central Florida Libraries. 21st Century Library. http://library.ucf.edu/21st/ (accessed June 1, 2018).
2 Florida Gulf Coast University. The Library NEXT Project. http://library.fgcu.edu/admin/renewal.html (accessed June 1, 2018).

John C. Hitt Library at Orlando FL campus

These changes and innovations include significantly downsizing print reference and other collections, relocating and redefining service points, reconfiguring public services, rethinking staffing models, adjusting subject librarian face-to-face activities, stepping-up online services, communicating with stakeholders, and keeping students and faculty in the loop so that their voices are heard and their needs met.

UCF LIBRARIES OVERVIEW

The University of Central Florida (UCF) is a research university that serves more than 66,000 students, making it one of the largest universities in the United States. UCF is home to 13 colleges that offer over 200 majors. It offers 95 bachelor's, 86 master's, and 31 doctoral degree programs, and ranks first among public universities in the nation for the annual number of baccalaureate degrees awarded and for the number of overall degrees conferred. UCF Libraries' collections include over 1.6 million print volumes. The John C. Hitt Library is UCF's premier library facility and is located on the main (Orlando) campus.

Architect's rendering of UCF 21st Century Library Project

Automated Retrieval Center exterior showing temporary covered bridge

UCF'S BUILDING RENOVATION PLAN

Construction work on UCF's 21st Century Library Project has been under way since fall 2016. The transformation of the John C. Hitt Library building includes the expansion and complete renovation of all five floors as well as improvements that include renovated elevators, stairwells, rest rooms, electrical outlets, and sprinkler systems. Renovations will also provide more group study rooms and graduate student areas, a digital commons, an expanded special collections and exhibits area, and a new main entrance.

An especially exciting element of Phase One (fall 2016–fall 2018) of this project is the construction of a four-story Automated Retrieval Center (ARC) on the north (Student Union) side of the library building. At full capacity, the ARC can hold 1.25 million volumes of the library's print collection. Books stored in the ARC will be requested with the click of a button in the online catalog, retrieved by one of the ARC's five robotic cranes, and be available for pickup at the Circulation Desk in minutes. Transferring books from the main library into the ARC will free up space for up to 1,600 additional user seats and student programming areas in the main library.

Many libraries worldwide, including over 20 in the United States, also have installed automated retrieval centers, including University of Chicago, North Carolina State University, University of Missouri Kansas City, and Georgia Southern University. Dematic Inc., is the company that installed UCF's ARC. The following videos demonstrate how this type of automated retrieval system is used in other academic libraries.

- Zach S. Henderson Library's ARC (Automated Retrieval Collection) (Georgia Southern University)
  - Video URL: http://www.youtube.com/watch?v=2JyC4qizkpw
- Santa Clara University Library—Automated Retrieval System (ARS)
  - Video URL: http://www.youtube.com/watch?v=ez9Z7rHqk1Y
- How RooBot the UMKC Libraries' Robot Works (University of Missouri, Kansas City)
  - Video URL: http://www.youtube.com/watch?v=8wJJLlTq7ts

- Macquarie University Library—Automated Storage & Retrieval System (Australia)
  - Video URL: http://www.youtube.com/watch?v=thKAS3CPz_c
- The New J. Paul Leonard Library: Book Retrieval System (San Francisco State University)
  - Video URL: http://www.youtube.com/watch?v=6hnAElubfIY
- Automated Book Delivery System & Virtual Browse (North Carolina State University)
  - Video URL: http://www.youtube.com/watch?v=p7q9u865SVk

Along with the completion of the ARC, a temporary library entrance with a temporary covered bridge will be created, at the ARC side of the existing library's main floor. This temporary entrance and bridge will provide a route through which books and other resources will be transported into the ARC during summer/fall 2018.

In the next phase of the 21st Century Library project, a building connecting the ARC to the existing library building will be completed and the top floor of the ARC will house a beautiful new student reading room.

EFFECTS OF THE NEW 5TH FLOOR QUIET ZONE ON THE MAIN FLOOR KNOWLEDGE COMMONS

The 5th Floor Quiet Zone, also part of the initial phase of the 21st Century Library project, opened on April 16, 2018, just in time for spring 2018 Finals Week study. This long- anticipated Quiet Zone, an area dedicated to individual study, research, and reflection, was the first area of the new library to open for student use. The space accommodates 170 seats, 85% of which are within an arm's length of electrical power. Each seat is designed for individual work, and, to preserve a quiet atmosphere, there is no group seating. Furniture selection was based on student testing and rating.

Even with a low-key "soft opening" of the new 5th Floor Quiet Zone during the week before spring final exams, students quickly filled every seat

John C. Hitt Library's 5th Floor Quiet Zone

John C. Hitt Library's 5th Floor Quiet Zone

of this area from day one. By day two, students were arriving at the library at 7:30 a.m. and camping out in the new area for the entire day.

When a fire alarm went off during the afternoon of the second day, students were reluctant to leave their seats in the 5th Floor Quiet Zone. Students correctly deduced that the fire alarm was a false alarm (due to construction work being done in some of the library's electrical closets), and they didn't want to give up their hard-earned seats, for fear of not regaining them when they were allowed back into the building.

What effects did the 5th Floor Quiet Zone opening have on the walk-in main level of the library, where the collaborative study Knowledge Commons (KC) is located? Almost immediately, there were far fewer students occupying

The 5th Floor of the John C. Hitt Library is now open for quiet study. Enjoy the peace and quiet! The new space now has over 160 seats, over 320 electrical outlets, and 40 brand-new desktop PCs.

Please Help Keep this new 5th floor Quiet Zone clean.
Thank you.

No Food | No Open Beverages | Lidded Beverages Permitted

Please help keep this new 5th Floor Quiet Zone clean. Thank You

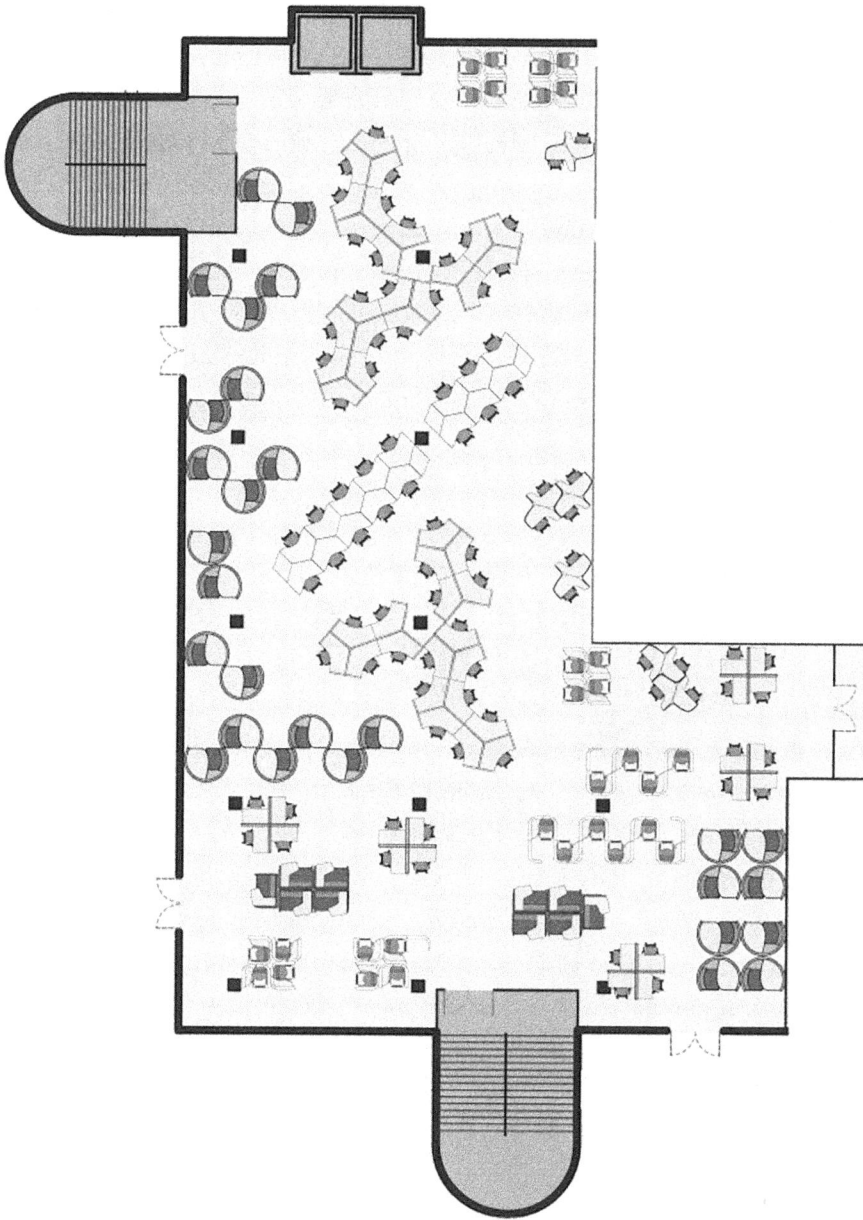

Floorplan of 5th Floor Quiet Zone

KC seats than usual at this busy time of the semester. Unless students had collaborative projects under way that required them to remain on the KC main level, the students seemed to vote with their feet and migrated to the new 5th Floor Quiet Zone.

Reference librarians staffing the Research Services Desk in the main floor knowledge commons area reflected that this spring 2018 final exam week was the smoothest, calmest, and least stressful that they'd experienced in the KC for many years. Due to the timely April opening of the 5th Floor Quiet Zone, we had the perfect solution for our over-crowded KC that usually was packed with students jammed shoulder-to-shoulder at tables or sitting on the floor. Also, there were few, if any, student complaints about noisiness in the KC, because now there was a perfect place for students seeking quiet study. A few student responses to the opening of the 5th Floor Quiet Zone on Facebook included: "UCF keeps getting better and better; introvert's paradise; it's a very nice study place!"

HOW THE BUILDING RENOVATION AND INGESTION OF ITEMS INTO THE ARC WILL AFFECT THE CURRENT MAIN FLOOR KNOWLEDGE COMMONS WHERE THE RESEARCH SERVICES DESK AND DEPARTMENT CURRENTLY ARE LOCATED

The plan is to begin the process of ingesting library collections into the ARC from the existing library building in fall 2018. When the ingestion begins, there will be a constant caravan of book trucks moving through the student-filled main floor KC—past the busy Research Services Desk, the Research Consultation cubicles, the Writing Center help cubicle, and student collaborative areas. Even though the book truck wheels will be treated with WD-40, it is anticipated that the movement of collections through the KC will create noise and commotion that will disrupt patron and staff activities.

In addition, the book truck routes through the KC and the creation of construction walls within the KC will infringe on space that previously had been devoted to student seating, student collaborative areas, and Research Service points. It is estimated that the library will temporarily lose a total of 504 seats. To partially compensate for this, the renovated 5th floor Quiet Zone, opened on April 16, 2018, added 170 seats.

Also, the Research and Information Services Department has been working to significantly downsize the main floor print reference collection. Since spring 2017, each subject librarian has been weeding the print reference

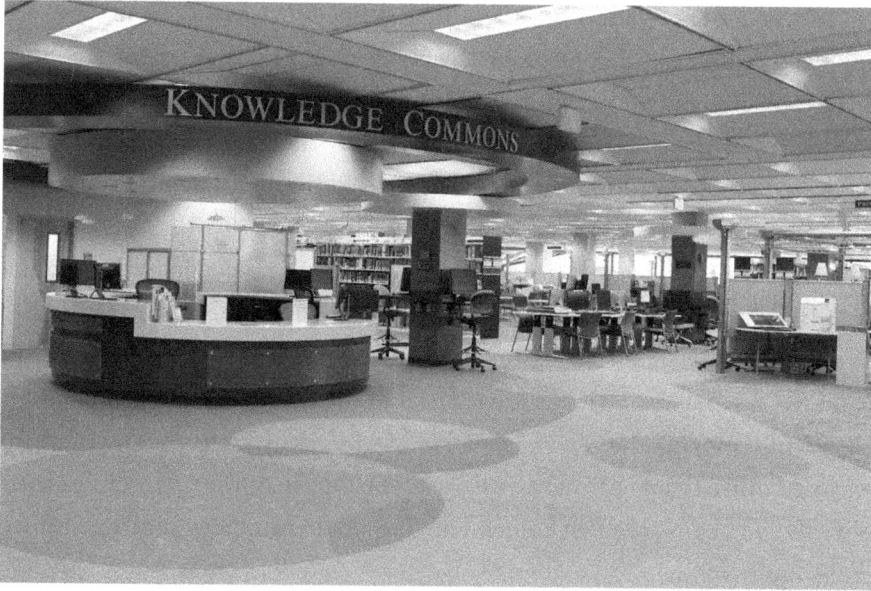

Main floor knowledge commons, John C. Hitt Library

collection areas within his or her assigned LC call numbers, with a goal of reducing the print reference collection by 75%. Most of these weeded reference volumes will be moved into the ARC. In the long term, the downsized print Reference Collection will allow more space for main floor student seating and collaborative activities.

BEYOND WD-40, EAR PLUGS, AND ASPIRIN . . . KNOWLEDGE COMMONS/RESEARCH AND INFORMATION SERVICES MAIN FLOOR CONTINGENCY PLANS

What will the Research and Information Services Department do if the 150+ day ingestion process winds up becoming too noisy to conduct reference conversations with patrons at the current Research Services Desk or to conduct one-on-one research consultations with patrons in the consultation cubicles adjacent to the desk? What if the noise is too loud for librarians to conduct "Ask a Librarian" virtual reference service within the main floor Research and Information Services Department office area, or the library is too noisy for librarians to work in their own offices?

To date, library administration has decided to take a "wait and see approach" with several contingency plans in their back pocket for reconfiguring public services, relocating and redefining service points, rethinking staffing patterns, adjusting subject librarian activities, and stepping up online services, if needed, during the periods that collections are being moved into the ARC.

For example, if needed, library administration is amenable to moving the main Research Services Desk service point away from the center of the KC to a desk shared with Circulation Services near the legacy main floor library entrance; moving research consultations into the library's enclosed main floor classrooms; moving the "Ask a Librarian (AAL)" virtual reference service into enclosed office spaces on another floor of the library or for AAL staff to temporarily work out of their homes; moving librarian offices into third floor group study rooms

TAKING UCF'S SUBJECT LIBRARIAN OUTREACH MODEL TO A NEW LEVEL POSSIBLY OUT OF THE LIBRARY ALTOGETHER

Since UCF's subject librarian program began in spring 2013, the subject librarians increasingly have been acting as their own CEOs with regard to outreach, research consultations, and library instruction. Currently most subject librarians are assigned only four-six hours per week of Reference Desk duties, with the rest of the desk slots being assigned to highly trained part-time adjunct librarians.

The subject librarians no longer are as tied to the Research Services Desk or their library offices as before, and their cell phones and newly issued lightweight Dell laptop computers are enabling them to be increasingly mobile. Some subject librarian strategies for avoiding the noisy library renovation areas include embracing more online activities (e.g., increased embedded librarianship, skyping, online research guides, and tutorials) to reach their students and faculty, or, getting out of the library altogether and working from other places on campus, such as the Faculty Center for Teaching and Learning or classroom buildings that house their assigned academic programs. Several of the subject librarians have created short "subject librarian welcome videos" to embed in their e-newsletters, research guides, database web pages, and e-mails.[3]

GETTING THE WORD OUT ABOUT RENOVATION MATTERS TO OUR CONSTITUENCIES

With so much change taking place in the library, we know that it is important to keep faculty and students in the loop so that their voices are heard and their needs are met during the long renovation period. Some of the communication strategies we are utilizing include conversations with stakeholders at Faculty Library Advisory Board and Student Library Advisory Board meetings, news updates on the libraries' website and social media outlets, signage on whiteboards at the library entrance and in the library elevators, "Installments Newsletters" in library restroom stalls, subject librarian e-newsletters and e-mails to academic departments, announcements at library instruction classes and workshops, and print flyers at service desks. A "21st Century Libraries" link http://library.ucf.edu/21st/ at the bottom of the libraries' home page provides a general overview and updates on this project, with tabs for "Recent News," "Renderings," "Plans," and "FAQ."

Also, one of the subject librarians has created a customized LibGuide titled "Automated Retrieval Center"[4] that provides detailed updates on this project with sections covering about the ARC; videos about ARC; construction information; currently; during initial move; after initial move; document delivery services; browsing online; current locations.

At each weekly library management meeting and at each monthly Research Services Department meeting details regarding the progress of this project are updated and are shared with the librarians to pass on to their assigned academic departments, faculty, and students.

Sometimes a little humor in library signage helps to smooth over renovation inconveniences.

---

3. University of Central Florida Libraries. Subject Librarian Sandy Avila Welcome Video. https://vimeo.com/ucflibraries/review/262842750/3c3ada2b59 (accessed June 1, 2018).
4. University of Central Florida Libraries. Automated Retrieval Center Research Guide. http://guides.ucf.edu/arc (accessed June 1, 2018).

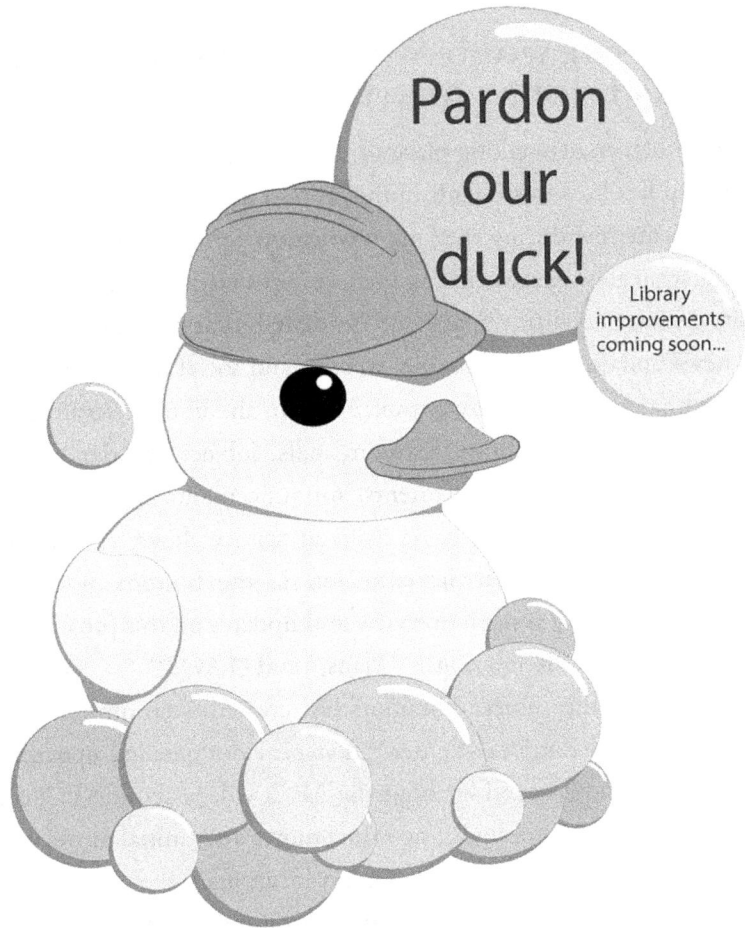

Pardon our duck!

Library improvements coming soon...

Please check this page for updates on dust, closures, and noise:

Information is posted at the entry to the library building, on signs in the elevators, and on signs throughout the building. When it has been indicated that an area is closed, please stay out. There are risks associated with entering those areas that are not immediately visible. Employees and work crews typically enter wearing hard hats and other protective gear.

Your cooperation enables the library project to progress as quickly as possible. We appreciate your understanding and offer a sincere apology for your inconvenience.

The Circulation Desk, at the entrance to the building, has earplugs if you are challenged by the noise.

REDEFINING REFERENCE SERVICES AND STAFFING AFTER THE NEXT PHASE OF THE RENOVATION PROJECT IS COMPLETED

The next phase of the renovation project (June 2018–June 2019) will be devoted to constructing the connector building between the ARC and the existing library building. When this phase has been completed, the current Research Services Desk probably will be replaced by a "one-stop-shopping integrated services" Information Desk located in the center of the KC, with the KC space previously used for librarian offices converted into student collaborative areas, and librarian offices being moved to the third floor.

The new Information Desk will serve as the primary point of first contact for patrons and will employ a tiered or triage staffing model that will utilize highly trained adjunct librarians, support staff, and student workers. These frontline information desk staff will be cross-trained to assist patrons by answering directional questions, providing technology troubleshooting, initiating basic reference help, and making informed referrals to subject librarians or Learning Commons partners. Information desk staff will provide expert guidance regarding a continuum or circle of services and will quickly and quietly skype the subject librarian on call when in-depth reference or other complex questions require the immediate attention of back-office professional staff.

ADVANTAGES OF TIERED OR TRIAGE STAFFING

Within this new model, subject librarians usually will not be stationed at the service desk during their designated reference shift, but instead will remain on call in their offices, ready to step in when in-depth research questions arise at the Information Desk. They will continue to provide scheduled one-on-one research consultations, library instruction classes, workshops, and outreach to their assigned academic departments and programs.

This tiered staffing triage model will add flexibility to the subject librarians' schedules, allowing them to work on information literacy class preparation, course-embedded instruction, creation of online research guides, collection development, committee assignments, and other professional responsibilities, instead of being tied to a service desk and devoting their time to lower-level inquiries.

STAFF TRAINING

Cross-training will be the strategy through which the part-time adjunct librarians, support staff, and student workers will attain proficiency, across functional units, to serve at the new Information Desk. This training will be delivered in a variety of ways, including staff meetings, shadowing, peer training, manuals, tutorial modules, and supervisor feedback. Also, easily available documentation (on the web or in desk manuals) will be important for troubleshooting the most common questions. An important part of the training will focus on when referrals are needed to subject librarians or to Commons partners.

Welcome to FGCU

FGCU AND LIBRARY BACKGROUND

As you drive on the campus of Florida Gulf Coast University (FGCU) in Fort Myers, Florida, you will see a large sign saying, "It started with Land and a Grand Plan." This summarizes the 20-year history of our university. In 1991, the former Florida Board of Regents recognized there was no state university serving Southwest Florida. Soon afterward, the governor signed legislation authorizing the tenth state university. The following year, local landowners offered more than 20 locations before the current site was selected. In 1993, the founding president was chosen, and plans for the campus were unveiled the next year. Our first student was admitted in 1997, and the first commencement ceremony was held the following year. The rest, as they say, is history.

Today we are a teaching university with 80% of our classes being taught by full-time faculty. FGCU has approximately 15,000 students with 92% from Florida. The university also has students representing 45 states and 85 countries. We have 54 undergraduate, 23 graduate, and 3 doctoral programs. In the past academic year, the top five awarded degrees were resort management, psychology, mass communication, business administration and management, and criminal justice.

The library began as a two-story building. Because Upsala College in East Orange, New Jersey, was closing, FGCU was able to purchase its library collection for the sum of $1 million. In 2006, a wing with four floors was added to the existing building. Today, the library is nearly 135,000 square feet. However, the fourth floor, which houses classrooms and faculty offices, does not belong to the library organization. This area is scheduled to undergo renovations by converting all of the faculty offices into classrooms.

The library follows the traditional organizational model, including departments such as Collection Management, Technical Services, Customer Services, Archives, and Systems. The Reference, Research, and Instruction Department, is home to seven subject librarians, an instructional technology librarian, an instructional support specialist, and a department head. The current department head is the first person hired specifically to serve as the department head.

THE COLLECTION ANALYSIS PROJECT

As expected, the original collection continued to grow and expand. After 17 years, a long overdue evaluation of the collection was necessary. There were two goals in mind. First, we needed to determine how the collection was utilized to ensure our users had the appropriate materials to support their educational and research needs. We also wanted to respond to changing space requirements such as student study and learning spaces.

To accomplish this evaluation, in 2014, the Collection Analysis Project (CAP) began. The plan was to have subject librarians use their subject expertise and program familiarity to identify items that still had merit and flag those items that were no longer needed. Our Collection Management staff would prepare detailed reports for the evaluations. The reports provided the subject librarians with information such as when an item was added to the collection, whether it had circulated in the past five years, and format. Throughout the project, subject librarians would work with faculty to assure them nothing would be removed from the collection that was critical to their research and teaching. Our dean also assured teaching faculty that if something was removed by mistake, we would repurchase those items.

HOW CAP WORKED

The CAP was accomplished over a two-and-a-half-year period with collection evaluations overlapping. For example, the Periodicals review happened parallel to the Reference collection review. The first collection reviewed was the VHS collection, which occurred during a two-month period. Because 82% of this collection had never circulated, we were confident in removing most of it and replacing the remaining items with streaming videos. Since the DVD/CD collection was very small, it only took two weeks to review. The next area was Periodicals, which took about six months to evaluate. Over the years we had switched many of our subscriptions to electronic versions, causing the print growth rate to slow to where we could consolidate two floors of bound periodicals onto one floor. The Reference collection also took six months to evaluate. During this review, our subject librarians determined what books would remain in reference, be moved to the General collection for circulation, transferred to remote storage site or be completely removed from the library. The review of the Microform collection was completed in stages over a year. The final collection evaluated was the General collection. During this review, which took 11 months, the subject librarians determined what books would remain in the General collection for circulation, would be transferred to remote storage site, or would be completely removed from the library.

With one final sweep of the Reference collection, the review was complete. We were able to consolidate and make a much smaller Reference collection. The General collection also was shifted and consolidated to accommodate the additional Reference materials.

MISSION ACCOMPLISHED

Our mission was accomplished. We reviewed the entire library collection to ensure it met the educational and research needs of our students and faculty. Overall, we removed 21% of the collection. Specifically, we removed 60% of the Reference collection with an additional 12% moving into the General collection. That was an overall reduction of 72% of the Reference collection. Our microform cabinets went from 50 cabinets down to 18. The remaining cabinets were moved out of the public area into Technical Services.

With all of these reductions, we opened large spaces throughout the building to create more student learning spaces. With end-of-year funding provided by the Provost, we made an initial purchase of new furniture. The new furniture created areas for students to work collaboratively or individually and created private spaces for subject librarians to conduct research consultations. After the installation of the initial purchase, we still had funds to obtain items we missed and more pieces of what the students liked and wanted. The additional furniture was chosen based on space requirements and student preference. The students are extremely happy with the new space designs. There's rarely an empty seat!

Reference collection before CAP

The Learning Commons today

Learning Commons from another view

Every seat taken!

LIBRARY NEXT: A CAMPUS CONVERSATION

This project was more than an analysis of our collection and opening spaces. It gave us the opportunity to reimagine the services we could offer. Therefore, we gave the entire project a more appropriate name, Library Next.

During the CAP, we wanted and needed input from our students and faculty. After all, we were creating the spaces for their use. A university-wide conversation called "Library Next: A Campus Conversation" was held. Librarians served as facilitators for three student-themed topics. One topic was to determine what students wanted to work independently and collaboratively. We wanted to know how the library could support their need for a quiet place for study while at the same time providing space to engage interactively. Another topic focused on library and academic support services. We were interested in finding out what we could do to help with student retention. We questioned if collaborating with other campus services, such as the Writing Center and the Center for Academic Achievement (both located in the library building), could help retain students. Our last student-themed topic focused on supporting new forms of learning and creating. We wanted to know what additional software or hardware was needed to support student learning.

Librarians also facilitated for two faculty and staff-themed topics. From the faculty and staff, we wanted information about instruction. The subject librarians were already using an integrated approach to teaching and assessing information literacy. We wanted to look for ways to work effectively with teaching faculty. We wanted to know if they were interested in holding office hours in the library so they could work directly with librarians and students who were conducting research. Our last faculty- and staff-themed topic focused on evolving the scholarly record and collections. We were interested in finding out what the library could do to make our virtual and electronic collections easier for faculty to integrate into their courses. We also wanted to promote and support open access and e-textbooks for our teaching faculty. As expected, we collected vast amounts of information from all who participated in our conversation.

LEARNING COMMONS TASK FORCE

We also initiated an internal task force made up of library faculty and staff. The task force was charged with making recommendations on creating a learning commons. Along with information gleaned from the "Campus Conversation," the task force surveyed the literature and interviewed leaders in the learning commons field. Their recommendations were presented to the dean and the entire library faculty.

WHERE WE ARE TODAY

Since the inception of Library Next, the subject librarians have continued providing research and instruction services. At times, this was not easy. Staffing was an issue requiring immediate attention. Just after the CAP began, the health sciences librarian departed. After a lengthy search, another librarian was hired. However, the gap left other librarians responsible for reviewing health sciences materials. In addition, there was not an instructional support specialist. While this individual did not directly participate in the CAP, she did provide support to the subject librarians. Hiring people to fill those positions was important to reimagining and extending our services.

With a fully staffed department, our librarians only needed to staff the Reference Desk about four to five hours a week. Librarians from other departments and part-time adjunct librarians are able to staff the remaining desk hours. With less time on the desk, subject librarians are able to put more emphasis on our chat and texting reference services. With additional advertising, our virtual reference statistics have nearly doubled in the past year. We are finding that more students are chatting with us within the library as they don't want to lose that comfortable seat! For the subject librarians, less desk time also means more time for research consultations and working with teaching faculty.

A mobile librarian service was initiated. This program provides service at the point of need. Everyone in the library who was interested participates. With tablets, we walk around the library looking for students in need. We recently added a mobile podium that serves as a focus point for the service. Students are directed to the podium from other service points when they need assistance in the stacks or other floors. We continue to enhance the service. We are working on a text feature that would allow service desk staff to directly contact the mobile librarian and tell him or her someone is coming for assistance.

The mobile librarian

The subject librarians have also worked with faculty to integrate their research guides into Canvas, our learning management system. With this addition, students have access to a research starting point as well as immediate access to their subject librarian. Likewise, some teaching faculty are so impressed with the research guides they want guides specific to their courses.

One of the items we learned from the "Campus Conversation" was how collaborating with other campus services could assist our students. As the collections shifted and spaces opened, we created the Hub. This is an area where our Center for Academic Achievement holds tutoring sessions. We have also partnered with the Writing Center to hold drop-in research clinics at least twice a semester. To date, attendance has been good. Of course, the free pizza probably helps.

Another item resulting from the Campus Conversation was the creation of a media production area. With more space, we were able to provide an area for this much-needed service. Collaborating with the campus radio station and Communications Department, we now house equipment for students to

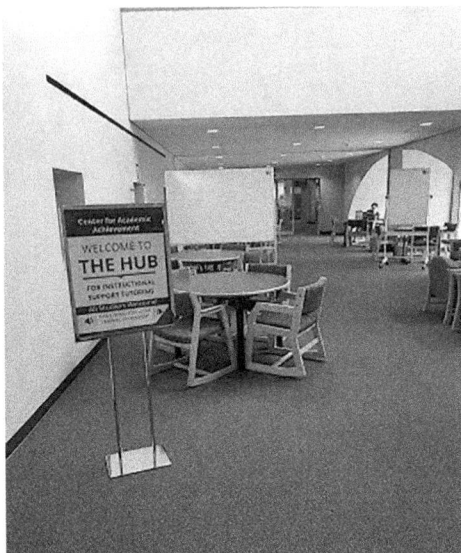

The Hub

create podcasts and other media activities. The Student Government recently approved additional funding for more equipment such as broadcast quality cameras, lighting, green screen frames, and acoustic paneling and curtains for sound absorption. The media production room was opened for student use in the spring. Once students receive an orientation to the room and its equipment, they are able to reserve the room whenever it is available.

Inside the media production room

FGCU FINAL THOUGHTS

As was stated at the beginning, "It started with Land and a Grand Plan." After 20 years as the only state university serving Southwest Florida, FGCU and its library continue with the grand plan to provide the highest quality and most innovative services to our students and faculty. With the CAP creating smaller, more functional collections and new spaces waiting to be filled with eager students, the door to reimaging new services has been opened. The library listened to our students, teaching faculty, and staff to expand our services to meet their research and teaching needs. In the next 20 years, no one knows what type of library services will be available. What is certain is that highly skilled and innovative library faculty and staff will provide those services.

COUNTER: RELEASE 5 OF THE CODE OF PRACTICE

Lorraine Estelle
COUNTER, lorraine.estelle@counterusage.org

ABSTRACT

Objective: The COUNTER Code of Practice first developed in 2003, is the international standard for reporting usage of scholarly content. In January 2019, Release 5 of the Code of Practice becomes effective. The development of the new release was undertaken by an expert group of volunteers who consulted with the wider knowledge community to ensure the needs of all stakeholders were met. The objectives of the development were consistency, clarity, simplification, flexibility, and continuous maintenance. This article describes how the new COUNTER reports and metric types work and explains how librarians can use them to answer common use cases and questions.

A BRIEF HISTORY OF COUNTER AND PREVIOUS CODES OF PRACTICE

In 2000, Richard Gedye, who at the time worked for Oxford University Press, was approached by the Association of Learned and Professional Society Publishers (ALPSP), who reported that the (PALS) (Publishers and Library Solutions) group wanted to develop a code of practice for usage statistics.[1]

---

1. The Publishers and Libraries Solutions (PALS) group was an organization created by the Jisc, the Publishers' Association (PA), and the Association of Learned and Professional Society Publishers (ALPSP).

Would Richard be prepared to form and lead a working group to bring some order to the area? Thankfully, he accepted the challenge and, after a thorough study of existing initiatives (most notably the International Coalition of Library Consortia (ICOLC) guidelines and the Association of Research Libraries E-Metrics project), convened an international meeting in London of some 50 specially invited experts from all sections of the information community, facilitated by consultants Bev Bruce and Judy Luther. An incredibly intensive and productive day-long session ensued, out of which emerged the basic structure of what became COUNTER's first Code of Practice, although the name COUNTER did not exist at that point. The meeting was critical for the success of the COUNTER project in at least two other ways. Firstly, it was an essential part of ensuring that all the key stakeholders were involved from the beginning. Secondly, it led to the discovery of people with key skills and knowledge, like Oliver Pesch from EBSCO, Marthyn Borghuis from Elsevier, David Sommer from Blackwell Scientific, Hazel Woodward from Cranfield University, Kathy Perry from the VIVA consortium, and Timo Hannay from Nature Publishing, who were working in the area and who went on to contribute generously and incredibly effectively to the successful transition of COUNTER from a research project to the authoritative body on usage statistics that it is today.

Nevertheless, it became apparent quite early on, that to achieve all its aims, COUNTER needed an investment in human resource that volunteers alone could not supply. The consequent appointment of Peter Shepherd as the project director was essential. Peter provided both the glue that kept all the constituent aspects of COUNTER working effectively together and the administrative energy that ensured it maintained the kind of momentum that quickly attracted over 100 publishers, vendors, and hosts to produce COUNTER-compliant usage reports and ensured that the codes evolved at an appropriate pace to keep up with changes in product development, information technology, and user behavior.

Although it is not apparent from the current COUNTER website,[2] the title of the organization was originally an acronym that stood for Counting Online Usage of NeTworked Electronic Resources.

---

2. http://www.projectcounter.org/

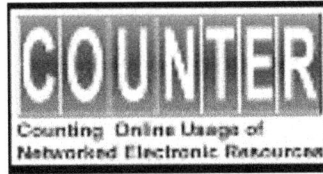

COUNTER published its first Code of Practice in 2003, setting the first international standard for reporting usage of scholarly content. COUNTER refined the code of practice to meet the evolving needs of its library, publisher, and vendor membership. By the time the second release was published in 2005, publishers were providing reports covering over 15,000 journals, as well as for databases and books. It became clear that manually collecting such a huge number of reports was time consuming and ultimately a barrier to libraries making effective use of the COUNTER reports. The problem was discussed with the National Information Standards Organization (NISO), and the result was the Standardized Usage Statistics Harvesting Initiative (SUSHI) standard, which enables libraries and library consortia to automate the retrieval of COUNTER usage reports.[3] SUSHI enabled the development of shared services, for example, JUSP (Journals Usage Statistics Portal), which offer all UK academic libraries a single point of access to journal, e-book, and database usage statistics, giving libraries a simple way to analyze usage trends and provide evidence of value for money.

COUNTER published Release 3 in August 2009, and Release 4 of the Code of Practice in December 2013, an integrated Code of Practice covering journals, databases, and books, as well as multimedia content.

THE OBJECTIVES FOR RELEASE 5

Release 4 went into effect in early 2014 and introduced several improvements over the prior releases, but by 2016 work was under way to further improve the reporting of usage of scholarly information in an ever-evolving digital environment. The challenge for Release 5 was to find the balance between addressing changing needs and reducing the complexity of the Code of Practice to ensure that all publishers and content providers can achieve compliance. The themes were consistency, clarity, simplification, flexibility, and continuous maintenance.

---

3. NISO SUSHI Standing Committee, NISO, url: http://www.niso.org/workrooms/sushi/ [accessed: 2018–07–05].

Consistency

Initially, COUNTER reports were spreadsheets intended for human consumption and were formatted for readability and understanding, but with the introduction of SUSHI in 2007, XML versions of reports were introduced for machine, rather than human consumption. The precision required for SUSHI resulted in inconsistencies between the XML and the spreadsheet versions of the reports.

Clarity

The various implementations of the Codes of Practices and supplementary documentation had resulted in a lack of clarity. Users of the Code of Practice encountered ambiguities that needed time-consuming clarification. Publishers and vendors and libraries found the number of metric types confusing and their names difficult to understand.

Flexibility

In Release 4 there were 23 reports. The objective was to replace these with fewer but more flexible reports allowing librarians to perform much more complex analysis, while also providing "standard" reports to address the common collection development needs.

Continuous Maintenance

History had shown that waiting five years between releases is too long, because publisher interfaces and technologies develop so quickly. New releases are also expensive for publishers to implement and in some cases a barrier to COUNTER compliance. Thus, an objective was to provide a mechanism for the community and the COUNTER Executive Committee to introduce updates to the Code of Practice without having to re-release the entire standard.

It is perhaps worth mentioning that Release 5 had also to deal with two other challenges. The first of these is known as the "Interface Effect." This occurs because some publisher interfaces, in improving the user experience, automatically present the user with the HTML version of an article. The user then has the option of selecting the article PDF. The result is that the full-text total download metric is incremented by two if a user looked at HTML that displayed automatically and then requested the PDF of the same article. Publisher interfaces that only display an abstract on an article landing page would have some users not choosing to look at the full text at all while others would select to view either HTML or PDF, but probably both. The first type of publisher platform would tend to have higher full-text request counts than the second type. Therefore, some librarians adjust Release 4 usage reports to compensate for the "Interface Effect" choosing only to use PDF counts when doing their cost-per-use analysis, which may result in discounting the value of the HTML version. The challenge for Release 5 was to develop new metrics, which would be independent of format and other user actions and thus less prone to the behavior of the user interface.

The second challenge was to improve book reporting. In Release 4, Book Report 1 and Book Report 2 are incompatible. Book Report 1 counts the number of times a user requested the full text of a book when the entire book is delivered in a single file. Book Report 2 counts the number of times a user requested a "section" of a book, where a section is, most usually but not always, a chapter. Within a given report, the metrics are usually comparable, a publisher will deliver books either as a single file or as sections, and the type of section is usually the same. However, trying to compare usage across platforms was problematic and librarians frequently asked how to deal with the fact that some vendors define a section as a chapter while others define it as individual pages, giving very different results. Librarians who wanted to do analysis and to report usage at a book title level were frustrated that the totals in BR1 and BR2 could not be added together. It was clear that a new metric was required representing unique book views within a session, to ensure that a book title is only credited with one "view," regardless of how many chapters, pages, or sections are viewed in a session.

THE DEVELOPMENT OF RELEASE 5

Following in the COUNTER tradition first established by Richard Gedye in 2000, a Technical Subgroup made up of expert volunteers from libraries, library consortia, publishers, and vendors was established. The members of the group who contributed their time and expertise were:

- Oliver Pesch, EBSCO Information Services, USA (Chair)
- Senol Akay, ACS, USA
- Daniel Albertsson, the Swedish University of Agricultural Sciences

- Irene Barbers, Forschungszentrum Juelich, Germany
- Simon Bevan, Cranfield University, UK
- Sarah Bull, UKSG, UK
- Andrew Goldthorpe, ABC (Audit Bureau of Circulation), UK
- Enrique Gonzales, AAAS, USA
- Kornelia Junge, Wiley, USA
- Sonja Lendi, Elsevier, Netherlands
- Tasha Mellins-Cohen, Microbiology Society, UK
- Paul Needham, Cranfield University, UK
- Bernd Oberknapp, Freiburg University Library, Germany
- Heather Staines, Hypothesis, USA

The Technical Subgroup held 32 meetings between January and July 2017 (approximately 330 person-hours). A further 660 hours was dedicated to the development of Release 5. However, input from the wider COUNTER membership and stakeholder community was essential in informing the final development. The first draft of Release 5 was published in January 2017 and feedback was sought from all stakeholders. During this 72-day consultation period, comments were gathered through a series of interactive webinars in English and German, at conference presentations and a structured survey. Stakeholders were also encouraged to provide unstructured feedback via e-mail.

The feedback received through these channels enabled the Technical Subgroup to refine and improve the Code of Practice. On 2 May, a revised draft was published, and additional feedback sought through more webinars and by e-mail. The Technical Subgroup used this feedback to further refine the Code of Practice prior to publication.

In July 2017, COUNTER published the Release 5 Code of Practice, which will be effective beginning January 2019. This lead time provides publishers and vendors with 18 months in which to implement the new Code of Practice.

ABOUT RELEASE 5

Master Reports and Standard Views

Four Master Reports are the foundation of COUNTER R5 Reports, one for each level in which usage is reported. Librarians will be able to use these

Master Reports to customize their analysis to meet specific reporting need. For ease of use, each of the Master Reports is associated with one or more summaries of types of activity, such as usage or access denials, called Standard Views.

Platform Master Report

All publishers and vendors must provide a Platform Master Report (PR) showing activity across all metrics for entire platforms. There is one Standard View for the PR:

- PR_P1: Platform Usage. A preset Standard View of PR showing total and unique item requests, as well as platform searches.

Database Report

Database Master Reports (DR) show activity across all metrics for entire databases or fixed collections of content that behave like a database. A DR can be filtered according to user needs and has two Standard Views:

- DR_D1: Database Search and Item Usage. A preset Standard View of DR showing total item investigations and requests, as well as searches.
- DR_D2: Database Access Denied. A preset Standard View of DR showing where users were denied access because simultaneous use (concurrency) licenses were exceeded, or their institutions do not have a license for the database

Title Master Report

A Title Master Report (TR) shows activity across all metrics for entire titles, which may be books or journals. The TR can be filtered according to user needs and has seven Standard Views, which apply to different Host Types. For example, a journal host does not need to provide TR_B1, which relates only to books. TR has an extra filter, Section_Type, in addition to the five that apply to all the Master Reports.

- TR_B1: Book Requests (excluding OA_ Gold). A preset book Standard View of TR showing full-text activity for all content that is not Gold Open Access. Numbers of Unique_Item_Requests As noted previously, in Release 4 it is not possible to compare e-book vendors reports, because these will vary based on whether the content is delivered as a complete book or by chapter, but the Unique_Title_Requests will be the same regardless of delivery mechanism.

- TR_B2: Book Access Denied. A preset book Standard View of TR showing where users were denied access to books because simultaneous use (concurrency) licenses were exceeded, or their institution did not have a license for the database e-book.

- TR_B3: Book Usage by Access Type. A preset book Standard View of TR showing all applicable metric types broken down by Access_Type. Used for aggregated Full Content e-book.

- TR_J1: Journal Requests (Excluding OA_ Gold). A preset journal Standard View of TR showing full-text activity for all content that is not Gold Open Access. Used for Aggregated Full Content e-journals.

- TR_J2: Journal Access Denied A preset journal Standard View of TR showing where users were denied access to journals because their institutions do not have a license for the content, or simultaneous use (concurrency) licenses were exceeded. Used for e-journals.

- TR_J3: Journal Usage by Access Type. A preset journal Standard View of TR showing all applicable metric types broken down by Access_Type. Used for Aggregated Full Content e-journals.

- TR_J4: Journal Requests by YOP (Excluding OA_Gold). A preset journal Standard View of TR breaking down the full-text usage of non-Gold Open Access content by year of publication (YOP). Used for Aggregated Full Content e-journal.

Item Master Report

An Item Master Report (IR) shows activity across all metrics for single items such as articles or videos; it is particularly useful for assessing usage from institutional repositories (an archive for collecting, preserving, and disseminating digital copies of the intellectual output of a research institution). IR can be filtered according to user needs and has two Standard Views:

- IR_A1: Journal Article Requests. A preset Standard View of IR showing total item requests for journal articles.

- IR_M1: Multimedia Item Request. A preset Standard View of IR showing total item requests for multimedia items.

Report Formats

The tabular versions of Release 5 reports have a common format. This same information will appear in the SUSHI version. The terminology used in reports is the same across reports and between the tabular and SUSHI version. Every COUNTER-compliant publisher and vendor must adhere to this common report format, as anything else will not be COUNTER compliant. A blank row was added before the body of the report in the tabular to afford easy filtering and sorting in Excel and Google Sheets.

METRIC TYPES

Usage

There are several different types of usage metric in Release 5, which break down into "investigations" and" requests." An investigation is tracked when a user performs any action in relation to a content item or title, while a request is specifically related to viewing or downloading the full content item.

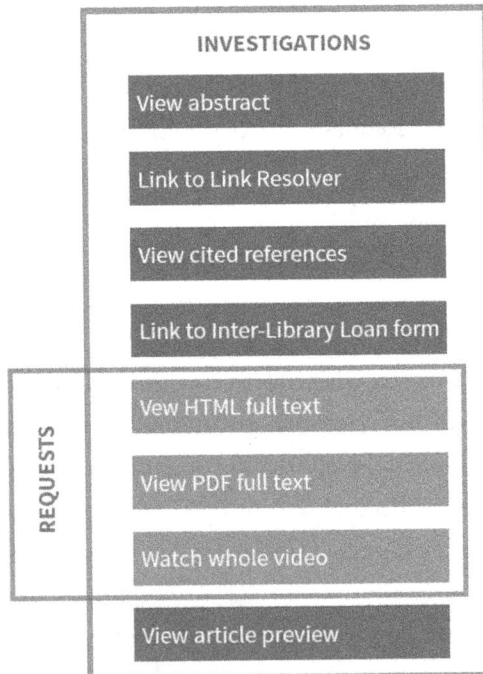

INVESTIGATIONS

View abstract

Link to Link Resolver

View cited references

Link to Inter-Library Loan form

REQUESTS

Vew HTML full text

View PDF full text

Watch whole video

View article preview

Investigations

- "Total_Item_Investigations": the total number of times a content item or information related to a content item was accessed.
- "Unique_Item_Investigations": the number of unique content items (e.g., chapters) investigated by a user.
- "Unique_Title_Investigations": the number of unique titles (e.g., books) investigated by a user.

Requests

- "Total_Item_Requests": the total number of times the full text of a content item was downloaded or viewed.
- "Unique_Item_Requests": the number of unique content items (e.g., chapters) requested by a user.
- "Unique_Title_Requests": the number of unique titles (e.g., books) requested by a user.

This following scenario created by Tasha Mellins-Cohen describes how user actions are reported using these metrics:[4]

SCENARIO

Susan is researching the history of antibiotics on Publisher Platform Alpha. From a list of search results she opens three article abstracts and a video record. All four records are different, but two of the articles are from the same journal.

The counts are:

- Total_Investigations: 4
- Unique_Item_Investigations: 4
- Unique_Title_Investigations: 3
- Total_Requests: 0
- Unique_Item_Requests: 0
- Unique_Title_Requests: 0

---

4. Tasha Mellins-Cohen, 2018. The Friendly Guide to Release 5 for Librarians. http://www.projectcounter.org/wp-content/uploads/2018/03/Release5_Librarians_PDFX_20180307.pdf [accessed: 2018–07–05].

After reading the abstracts, Susan downloads the PDFs for two of the articles, both from the same journal. The counts change to:

- Total_Investigations: 6
- Unique_Item_Investigations: 4
- Unique_Title_Investigations: 3
- Total_Requests: 2
- Unique_Item_Requests: 2
- Unique_Title_Requests: 1

To calculate cost-per download, the librarian should use the two Unique_Item_Requests.

Searches

There are four different types of search metrics in Release 5:

- "Searches_Regular": the number of times a user searches a database, when he or she has actively chosen that database from a list of options, or there is only one database available to search.
- "Searches_Automated": the number of times a user searches a database, when he or she has not actively chosen that database from a list of options. That is, Searches_Automated is recorded when the platform offers a search across multiple databases by default, and the user has not elected to limit his or her search to a subset of those databases.
- "Searches_Platform": the number of times a user searches a database, regardless of the number of databases involved in the search.
- "Searches_Federated": the number of times a search is run remotely by a computer.

Access Denials

These are metrics are also known as turnaways. Two types of access denial metric are tracked and reported in Release 5:

- "No_License": counted when a user is unable to access a unique content item because his or her institution does not have a license to the content.

- "Limit_Exceeded": counted when a user is unable to access a unique content item because his or her institution's cap on the number of simultaneous users has been exceeded.

Elements and Attributes

Release 5 has added a series of elements and attributes to the standing metrics. These help to provide much more detailed information in an organized way. The new elements and attributes are:

- "Data_Type": used to group content at the level of the title.
- "Section_Type": used when Data_Types are delivered in small subunits (e.g., journal articles).
- "Access_Method": applies when a host allows Text and Data Mining (TDM) of its content and can distinguish TDM activity from all other activity.
- "YOP": Year of Publication: the four-digit year in which the Version of Record was published.

SUSHI FOR COUNTER RELEASE 5

Release 5 supports the latest version of SUSHI, which adopts a RESTful interface returning JSON-formatted usage. This is in line with modern web development, using approaches that are familiar to most web developers. It allows retrieval of full reports or snippets of usage, and allows usage display to be embedded in other applications.

COMMON USE CASES AND COMMON QUESTIONS

Journal Usage

Perhaps the most common user case is to use COUNTER reports to calculate cost per use. The Standard View *TR_J1: Journal Requests (Excluding OA_Gold)* will enable librarians to do this easily. The report contains the usage for licensed content and excludes usage of Gold Open Access articles. This is important because librarians want to perform cost-per-use calculations on the articles they have paid for, and to exclude articles paid by the authors or authors' funders. The key metric type is "Total_Item_Requests."

Journal Usage for Back Files and Perpetual Access

This user case is about separating out usage and cost per use when the same journal title is accessed under two separate licenses. The first license covers current content, and the second license covers backfiles of the journal (very often retrospectively digitized). The Standard View *TR_J4: Journal Requests by YOP (Excluding OA_Gold)* enables this. The report Journals contains usage for licensed content broken out by Year of Publication (YOP) and excludes usage of Gold Open Access articles. The key metric type is "Total_Item_Requests," and librarians can filter the results by title to view usage by YOP or create pivot tables.

Database Usage

The Standard View *DR_D1 Database Search and Item Usage* enables librarians to examine usage by searches, requests, and investigations. The key metric types are "Total_Item_Investigations" (for non-full-text databases) and "Total_Item_Requests" (for full-text databases).

Comparable Book Usage

The Standard View *TR_B1: Book Requests (excluding OA_ Gold)* enables librarians to examine usage whether the platform delivers whole books or individual chapters. The report contains the usage for licensed content and excludes usage of Gold Open Access content. The key metric type is "Unique_Title_Requests."

Compliance

To become COUNTER compliant, publishers and vendors must engage an independent accountant to audit their COUNTER reports within six months of signing the Declaration of COUNTER Compliance and annually thereafter. COUNTER will accept an audit done by any certified public accountant (USA), by a chartered accountant (UK), or by their equivalents in other countries. Alternatively, the audit may be done by the COUNTER-approved auditors listed on the COUNTER website. Very small publishers may request permission to be audited every other year. All publishers and vendors who have passed their audits are listed on the COUNTER website. Many librarians complained previously that some publishers declared themselves COUNTER compliant and used the COUNTER logo, when in fact they were not compliant at all. To deal with this, a publisher passing the independent COUNTER audit for Release 5 will now be issued with a dated logo confirming its COUNTER compliance. If they display this logo on their website, it must link back to their entry on the COUNTER website, where librarians will be able to see the date of their last successful COUNTER audit and the scheduled date for the next audit.

ONGOING WORK TO SUPPORT RELEASE 5

Release 5 will be effective from January 2019, but COUNTER cannot rest on its laurels. It is focused on helping publishers and vendors to become compliant, by answering their queries and by providing supporting guides and webinars. However, even with this assistance it is important to ensure that the rates of interoperability and compliance are as high as possible. Thus, COUNTER is developing a web-based Validation Tool that will test compliance of COUNTER Release 5 Master Reports and Standard Views, delivered in tabular format, or delivered in JSON via the COUNTER_SUSHI API. The Validation Tool will enable publishers and vendors to test their implementation of the COUNTER_SUSHI API and COUNTER Release 5 Reports during the development process, ensuring errors are caught and corrected before release. The tool will be made freely available on the web for all to use.

Release 5, to the consternation of library consortia managers, eliminates consortium reports because their size makes creating and consuming them impractical. To address this, COUNTER is creating Release 5 Consortium Harvesting Tools. These tools should enable consortia to automate the harvesting of COUNTER Release 5 Report for member libraries.

STREAMLINING ACCESS TO CONTENT IN A ONE-CLICK WORLD: RA21 PILOTS BALANCE RESEARCHER PRODUCTIVITY AND USER PRIVACY

Todd A. Carpenter
Executive Director, National Information Standards Organization (NISO), tcarpenter@niso.org

Ann Gabriel
Vice President, Academic & Research Relations, Elsevier, a.garbriel@elsevier.com

Robert Kelshian
Director of Access Services, American University Library, calvin@american.edu

Don Hamparian
Senior Product Manager, Identity Management and EZproxy, OCLC, hamparid@oclc.org

Members of the RA21 Steering Committee

ABSTRACT

The Resource Access in the 21st Century (RA21) project is a joint NISO-STM Association effort to improve the user experience of using federated identity services to access digital resources. As users have grown more mobile and less tethered to physical network access, the means of authenticating users has remained static for most institutions. RA21 attempts to address the Where Are You From problem by storing hints about library patron's preference of identity provider service in order to facilitate the authentication process. In order to keep this process secure and privacy-protecting, the project also recommends limited metadata about the user be sent to provide access.

There has been a revolution in how content has been delivered to library patrons over the past three decades. It has not happened in the blink of an eye but has transpired over some 25 years. We collectively have moved from an era when the majority of content purchased and delivered from publisher to library then onto patrons has shifted from primarily print into primarily electronic content, especially for journal content, but for reference works and many forms of books as well. During this time, scholarly publishers and libraries have relied primarily on the same form of access control for this online content.

At the outset of the delivery of content via the Internet in the early 1990s, it became obvious quickly that usernames and passwords were a poor method of providing secure access to content. Not only was it required to have a username-password combination for every resource, to keep access secure, every user would need a username and password combination. Managing this structure at scale would have been a near-impossibility. This led libraries and publishers to quickly move to adopt Internet Protocol (IP) address authentication systems to provide access. The IP address system is a protocol used to manage networks by assigning each network a digital location address and each device on a network subdomain address, such as http://192.1.168.4 or http://104.27.187.14. At the time, in the early 1990s, one could reasonably presume that if a device was located on a particular network, that the user of that device was authorized to be on that network, since most people accessed the Internet via desktop computers that had to be physically attached to networks. Therefore, using the IP address system to validate someone's right to gain access to subscribed digital content made sense. By allowing a range of IP addresses to gain access, the publisher and the library could provide reasonably secure access to all of the computers attached to the campus (or business, or library) network, without each user having to login individually as they moved from service to service.

This system worked reasonably well at first. There were issues with managing IP addresses as networks became more decentralized and the number of networks expanded. As devices became smaller and more mobile, the problems of providing access via IP address authentication became more numerous. Users became untethered from their networks. As devices became more powerful and smaller, patrons began demanding access to library resources from their homes, from coffee shops, from anywhere they could get a cellular Internet connection. To accommodate these users, libraries implemented systems, proxy servers, that could provide a tunnel access point that would allow users to validate on the network and then appear to the publisher's systems as if the user was on the library's network.

This system of proxy servers also worked reasonably well. However, proxy servers had several problems. First, proxy servers are a tantalizing target for those who wish to compromise a network for nefarious purposes. Initially, compromised credentials might be used to download untold volumes at once, until a publisher noticed and cut off access to the library's proxy server. Now, more sophisticated attacks take place where only a limited number of materials are taken, occasionally on demand, which might slip under the radar of a publisher's security protocols. Regardless, the publisher's only recourse has been to shut down the entire proxy server until the compromised credentials are identified and reset. This could lead to the publisher shutting down off-network access for the library's entire patron base until the situation is corrected. Hundreds of librarians have reported having to deal with this situation on a recurring basis.

In addition, the current system provides librarians with a woefully inadequate data on patron's use of library resources. Usage data is available only at an aggregate level, and normally on downloads only. Rob Kelshian, director of Access Services, American University Library, described the variety of challenges he faces at his library. While through turnaway data, it is possible to identify content that users might want but do not have access to, but it is difficult to discern how often users can't get to what the library does subscribe to, but can't access for other reasons. At American University, a large and growing percentage of access is happening from off-campus locations and not directly through the campus network. Additionally, an increasing number of library patrons engaging in the library's resources are participating in remote programs, and thus they never engage directly with the library or its staff. Through the American University network, patrons have both a Shibboleth login service and an EZproxy server. The majority of library usage is through the proxy, because of its broader adoption by publishers and the challenges of implementing it because of user interface barriers. Rather than passing first to content, the patron has to be aware of the need to first navigate through the authentication website, which is a barrier to access. The library administration is asking itself, is the institution getting the most for its investment, if it is not doing its utmost to ensure access is provided to resources the library subscribes to? In this environment, the library at American University and its staff are committed to protecting user privacy. Often the library staff are more committed to privacy than the users themselves. There is a hope that an approach could be found that addresses both of these needs.

It should be noted that the EZproxy system marketed by OCLC is not "hacked" or compromised at a system level. The underlying technology is stable and secure. The most common problem, by far, is compromised credentials at the institution. OCLC recommends a four-part strategy to secure access to the system through proper configuration; prompt detection and closure of compromised credentials; education of the institutional administration, content providers, and users; as well as interorganizational collaboration to secure the network. Configuration of the systems requires time and resources on a regular basis to ensure the system is functioning optimally. The simplest and most impactful change that libraries could implement are educational campaigns around patron's use of passwords and basic security. This extends to publishers and other holders of sensitive data, but the primary source of breached systems are the users of that system and their careless approach to or management of passwords. Beyond that, there is an awareness that access control should be made more secure and more robust. As such, OCLC has been an active participant in several initiatives to improve access including the RA21 initiative and is committed to supporting the output of the RA21 initiative. They have acknowledged that they may incorporate an RA21 recommended approach in the service it provides, or other services.

With all the work-arounds surrounding the use of IP access control systems, this entire technology stack is still not providing the patron with a very effective user experience. Because of the nature of library access to content, where a user can come from nearly any website, search engine, or online resource, and expecting to be seamlessly linked to content from nearly any other subscribed resource, the potential options for access control points are limitless.

The university technology community in the mid-2000s developed a security protocol built around the Security Assertion Markup Language (SAML), which is a structure for communicating authentication and authorization data between identity providers (IDPs) and publishers. This system is robust in its ability to share information about users either anonymously or with more detailed demographic information, or even personally identifiable information. The system around SAML was built with many different use cases and is therefore not built with "privacy by design," as modern systems might be, because there are some institutional application use cases where the identity of the user must be known to provide the service, such as in the case of course management software. Simply because the system has the capability for sharing personally identifiable information about the user does not mean that it cannot be privacy-protecting. One of the first use cases for SAML-identity management systems was library use cases where privacy was a key factor. The SAML system as it has been deployed in institutions around the world also has the capability to function in a truly anonymous fashion through the use of access-control tokens, which contain no information about the patron. All that is required to provide access are the attributes that this is an authenticated user from this institution for this set time period.

In the fall of 2015, members of the Pharma Documentation Ring, a group of pharmaceutical industry libraries, reached out to the Copyright Clearance Center (CCC), in an attempt to begin a dialogue with the publishing community seeking to improve the access control system in place for subscribed access to scholarly content. These pharmaceutical companies faced difficulty with the default status of IP access to content because of the distributed, ever-changing, worldwide nature of their workforces. Pharmaceutical companies are also particularly concerned about security of their networks and the risks posed by compromised access. They sought an improved method for access control that was more secure and more robust than what was currently being provided. The CCC subsequently passed along this request to the International STM Association who convened a group of publishers to discuss improving the situation. This group quickly realized that any project to improve the broader network of authentication would require the involvement of both the library and publisher communities. The Universal Resource Access project, specifically focused on the pharmaceutical community, was launched to explore the corporate-specific issues at play regarding access control. A broader conversation was begun around improving the larger technology stack that supports access control for all scholarly communications, which took shape into the Resource Access for the 21st Century (RA21) project. While initially begun at the International STM Association, it was at this stage the National Information Standards Organization (NISO) was brought into the conversations as a way to expand the participation—particularly from libraries—in this initiative. The project was approved as a joint NISO-STM Association by the NISO members and the Board of the STM Association initiative in February 2017. A working group was formed with representation from many of the leading scholarly publishers, librarians, and technology companies. That group began its work in April 2017.

The RA21 initiative quickly settled on several principles. These included that the project would seek to provide patrons the access to all content from any location on any device of their choosing. They should be able to begin from any entrance point and reach their desired content with the minimal amount of interaction. Publishers and technology providers should provide a consistent user interface to simplify adoption from users. The resulting protocol should be able to provide the user with reliable privacy, while improving security and allowing for greater personalization, should the user so choose. Furthermore, there was agreement that any proposed solution should be open and available to all users without fee. The solution should not be proprietary and should be reasonably easy to implement. As an open standard, the solution must be vendor neutral and not subject to an industry monopoly that could control the system. Because the solution should need to be functional across all institutions of various sizes and technological expertise levels, the solution should not create tremendous amounts of new work, significant implementation costs, or tremendous amounts of ongoing maintenance. Knowing that every institution would not be in a position to adopt the solution quickly, the best practice should allow for gradual implementation and an overlapping of implementable solutions over a protracted period.

The project sought to develop several approaches to address the problem using a SAML-based approach. Other foundational technologies were initially considered, such as OpenID and the Initiative for Open Authentication (OATH). It was determined that while these other technologies might be appropriate solutions to the problems the community currently faces, nothing is as widely adopted among both institutions and content providers as federated identity services based upon SAML. It made the most sense that if a solution was to be adopted relatively quickly, it would be based on the existing technology, not on new approaches that have not yet seen wide deployment in the institutional, library, and publisher communities. While it was acknowledged that these other services might be easier for smaller institutions to deploy, or might have easier implementation paths, once widely implemented, rather than focusing on the "next new technology," the group decided to try to build on and improve on the very wide adoption of SAML and federated identity services.

User privacy is one of the guiding principles of the RA21 initiative, and it was enshrined as one of the goals of the project. In addition to the industry commitment to privacy, the General Data Protection Regulation from the EU is also as powerful driver with regard to the privacy expectations of the project. Most publishers are already working toward integrating the GDPR in their business processes, and a new authentication system will need to be compliant with GDPR privacy rules. The SAML federated authentication technology has in-built mechanisms for preserving privacy if properly implemented by the institution. The institution is fully in control of what personally identifiable information is disclosed to a content provider, not the publisher. Academic SAML Identity Providers provide unique, persistent, but opaque identifiers to identify a user, and these identifiers need not provide any personally identifiable information to provide access. However, it is possible for publishers to ask for additional personal information from users via a registration processes to provide personalized services, but this is completely up to the user and would be governed through the disclosure of the publisher's privacy policies. In this way, users can control whether to expose their information or not based on their privacy interests. However, this is not a requirement of the RA21 or SMAL system, and access can be provided anonymously.

The RA21 initiative was initially comprised of three pilots, the Universal Resource Access (URA) corporate pilot, and the two academic pilots, a cloud-based Where Are You From (WAYF) and a Privacy Protecting Persistent WAYF (P3W). The corporate URA project explored the difficult challenges that are unique to the pharmaceutical industry and its provision of corporate identity credentials. The URA project explored many options and is considering the deployment of an identity federation to manage these credentials in the way that many academic institutions do. The two academic pilots sought to address the problem of gathering enough information from the user to easily determine which identity provider credentials should be directed to, since there are hundreds of them, and they are not often easily identified with the institutions that participate in them. In some ways, this is a metadata problem, in which the network is broadly aware of which institutions are participating in which identity federation. A second element of this problem is making the system retain enough information so that it does not have to prompt the patron to provide information about which identity provider should be validating their login credentials.. This problem, known as the Where Are You From (WAYF), is the core question that the RA21 sought to address. The cloud-based WAYF pilot envisioned a cloud-based registry of devices that associated a device with an identity provider and then passed information from the user to the publisher about which identity provider that device should be directed to. The P3W project would be built around "WAYF hints" that would be stored in the browser after a user visits his or her respective identity provider (IdP) that could be used in the future to redirect the user to that identity provider's service again, without having to query which is the appropriate IdP repeatedly.

The RA21 project made significant progress through the spring and summer of 2018. The working group completed an evaluation of two pilots, the WAYF Cloud and the P3W, each of which offered alternative technical approaches to identity provider persistence. The evaluation involved a detailed technical evaluation by the architects of both pilots and an in-depth security and privacy analysis by a Security and Privacy subgroup team. The security review followed the Microsoft STRIDE Threat Classification Model, commonly used for analyzing threats from six standard categories:

- **S**poofing of user identity
- **T**ampering
- **R**epudiation
- **I**nformation disclosure (privacy breach or data leak)
- **D**enial of service
- **E**levation of privilege

Both pilots would need to follow best common security practices if deployed, such as regular auditing and penetration testing, security of the server and API components, which are core to their baseline ranking, but it was anticipated that best practices would be applied to both over the long term. The

P3W solution provided a lower level of risk exposure according to these six categories, primarily because of the distributed nature of the stored data.

To assess the data privacy risks, the privacy and security team conducted a data protection impact assessment ("DPIA") to analyze potential issues based on GDPR requirements. The DPIA is an analysis of expected processing activities related to their potential privacy impacts. The analysis includes details of the processing activity itself as well as an assessment of the risks associated with those processing activities and any measures that should be taken to mitigate those risks.

While it was determined that both the cloud-based and the browser-based pilots were successful in testing technical approaches to identity provider persistence, the browser-based Privacy Preserving Persistent WAYF solution was selected to advance for development into an operational service. The rationale for this was that the browser-based solution was less complicated, required less coordinated investment, and provided fewer attack vectors, should one desire to attempt to create mischief with the system. The P3W approach minimizes the amount of data held in a single place, thereby minimizing potential security or privacy breaches based on the STRIDE and DPIA analysis that were conducted. Additionally, the browser-based approach does not centrally store any information about patrons, their devices, nor their activity, which reinforced the privacy goals of the project. All the information that is stored using the P3W approach is information stored on the patron's device about his or her preference of institutional identity provider. As such, the information is in the user's control—they could delete it at any time if they desired to—and is very limited as a target of compromise both because it will be securely encrypted for only a single device. Even if the data were compromised in some fashion, the data stored is of minimal value, since the information stored is not the user's credentials, nor the identity tokens used to access content via SAML, but only the preference of where these credentials should be sent to. The P3W architecture offered a functionally equivalent service to the WAYF Cloud architecture, but with no central collection of information thus adhering to the privacy principle of data minimization.

It is also clear that the technology that underpins this infrastructure is not the only component of its eventual success. There will need to be a unified user experience implemented across the vast majority of content providers, so that users at any institution can know what to expect and how to navigate to their appropriate identity provider using the RA21 P3W locally stored preferences. Another subgroup of the project is working on development of a common user interface, which can be shared as a part of the overall RA21 recommended practice. Furthermore, there is an adoption and education component of the group's work, which is being managed by a second subgroup.

The subcommittee has published, as part of the output of the project, the security and privacy review with complete sets of the criteria reviewed. It is anticipated that by the end of 2018, the entire recommendation will be publicly available. The leadership of the RA21 initiative is exploring the infrastructure and service provision needs of maintaining the open source code, the JavaScript libraries necessary to make the P3W service function, an ongoing production service that operates the JavaScript code, and the maintenance of the service on an ongoing basis. Once the RA21 service is publicly available, there will be a need for ongoing governance of the project and its outputs, as well as publicity and training for the community on how to implement the RA21 technology locally at both publishers and libraries. Both NISO and the International STM Association are committed to the long-term viability of the initiative and are exploring ways to sustainably support the work after it is published. As currently envisioned, this could take the form of an industry consortium that supports these ongoing elements, with technology, governance, education, and promotion being handled either collectively or separately by consortium members.

The RA21 project's ultimate goal will be to advance a simpler approach to access control that is more robust than the current method of IP-based authentication. It is anticipated that by simplifying the user of identity federations, they can become more reliable and useful methods of access control for most users. This will align the publishing industry more closely with widely adopted practice for authentication and authorization among academic institutions. This will make the user experience more simple, will make the access control systems more secure, and will improve the potential for assessment of the use of library resources.

STATISTICAL ANALYSIS, DATA VISUALIZATION, AND BUSINESS INTELLIGENCE TOOLS FOR ELECTRONIC RESOURCES IN ACADEMIC LIBRARIES

Cheng Cheng
Acquisitions & Electronic Resources Librarian, SUNY Oneonta, cheng.cheng@oneonta.edu

Tracy Gilmore
Senior Assessment Librarian, California State University Long Beach, tracy.gilmore@csulb.edu

Colleen Lougen
Electronic Resources Librarian, SUNY New Paltz, lougenc@newpaltz.edu

Connie Stovall
Assistant Director for Strategic Research & Analysis, Virginia Tech, cjstova@vt.edu

ABSTRACT

Most academic libraries spend a significant amount of their total expenditure budget on electronic resources. While they are high-value assets for modern libraries, the expensive annual subscription cost and continuing price increases of e-resources also make them a substantial budgeting burden. It is therefore essential to have a clear statistical view of the trends and patterns for e-resources and to conduct evidence-based decision making based on those trends and patterns. This chapter will focus on business intelligence tools available for this type of analysis, including Excel and Redlink, and Tableau, and will include a comparative analysis. The evaluation of each BI services will be based on ease-of-use, data analytics, visualization, dissemination, and service support. In addition to discussing the pros and cons of each tool, we will demonstrate how each tool displays visualizations and dashboards. Secondly, the chapter will discuss the methodology applied in a statistical analysis and data visualization research project, as well as business trends and patterns in the field of libraries' e-resources.

INTRODUCTION

More than ever, academic libraries place great importance on using vast amounts of data and robust analyses and visualizations to aid in evidence-based decision making and demonstrating impact. A primary impetus for the careful evaluation of electronic resource collections hinges on the ongoing compression of academic library budgets, which has been noted for several years in numerous surveys. For example in the 2016 *ACRL Academic Library Trends and Statistics*, a significant portion of the libraries surveyed received budget decreases (19%) or sustained flat budgets (60%) (Bosch, Albee, and Henderson 2018, 29). Meanwhile, prices for electronic resources and serials keep rising with an average of 6% increases per year since 2012 (Bosch, Albee, and Henderson 2018, 28). Allen Powell (2011) of EBSCO Publishing noted the "significant gap" between the budgets of academic libraries and the accelerating costs of scholarly information or the "serials crisis" (107–108). Hence, collecting, analyzing, and translating data into a visual narrative is becoming progressively vital in evaluating the return on investment of the ever-increasing cost of electronic resources. Business intelligence (BI) tools make taking on these tasks much more manageable.

BI tools offer advantages to librarians as these resources continue to proliferate, as more data becomes available, and as librarians are tasked with presenting data to convey trends and actionable insights to multiple audiences. According to *PC Magazine*, some of the best BI tools for 2018 include the following: Zoho Reports, IBM Watson Analytics, Microsoft Power BI, Tableau Desktop, Sisense, Domo, and Google Analytics (Baker 2017). Beyond *PC Magazine*'s recommendations, many consider Microsoft Excel to be a BI tool, especially considering many of its newer features that allow users to create visually appealing dashboards. Lastly, industry-specific tools exist, like Redlink, which is a BI tool developed for libraries and publishers. In short, many BI tools are available but occur with great range in cost and requisite skills. Importantly, what they all do centers on allowing users to manipulate, analyze, and report on massive amounts of data via visually effective means, such as interactive dashboards and graphic visualizations.

Transforming raw data into compelling visual displays that assist in effectively communicating and interpreting a library's value and story is an increasing need (Magnuson 2016). Specifically for electronic resources, it helps librarians decide which subscriptions to renew or cancel. The trouble lies in the glut of information available, the structure in which it is available, and utilizing that glut quickly and effectively. Many academic libraries download or have access to hundreds of COUNTER (Counting Online Usage of Networked Electronic Resources) Reports, which amounts to tens of thousands of lines of information about electronic resource usage, but handing over a spreadsheet with 40,000 lines of data is not an effective way to communicate to library deans—much less provosts—the value of those subscriptions. Further, such spreadsheets do not allow library liaisons or collection development librarians to drill down easily into data, for example, by publisher, year, or user group in a dynamic, visually appealing manner. In "An Overview of Information Visualization," the author asserts the importance of visualizations:

> Human vision is highly selective when it comes to different sizes, shapes, colors, spatial positions, and so on, and that is what makes human vision a powerful tool for data analysis and interpretation. By organizing and presenting data in a carefully designed, selective way, one can exploit human vision to gain different interpretations and understandings from the data. Additionally, vision helps extend memory and cognitive capacity, both of which play a significant role in how people process information. (Chen 2017, 6)

Given the profound amount of electronic resources data and the importance of visually depicting its value, especially when electronic resources spending often makes up close to half of a library's total budget, turning to and investing in BI tools to aid with visualizations and analysis makes sense.

Numerous BI tools exist, and here the authors discuss three options: one that is ubiquitous (Excel), the second that is industry-specific (Redlink), and the third (Tableau), which is a top-rated but a more expensive choice. These BI tools represent the spectrum of pricing and licensing options, and all are fairly widely used by assessment and other academic librarians. Each is briefly summarized herein. Further, use scenarios are presented for three different universities.

Excel

Excel is one of the most widely used BI tools for analyzing and visualizing data. For librarians who manage large amounts of usage and statistics data, one of Excel's many advantages is its familiarity and accessibility. For example, Kilb and Jansen (2016) used BI tools, such as Excel, to calculate the return on investment (ROI) for "Big Deal" e-journal packages at the University of North Carolina at Chapel Hill. Staff used the cost-per-use (CPU) data to identify e-journals that were in need of closer review and ultimately created robust visualizations to share with campus stakeholders and vendors to renegotiate their "Big Deal" contract (194). The Collection Assessment Team at Virginia Tech University Libraries uses Excel extensively to communicate information about online resources in visual, interactive reports. Creating dashboard-style reports in Excel transforms the COUNTER data and other vendor-provided reports into clear visual statements that provide meaning to multiple audiences.

To support the data audience at Virginia Tech with actionable information and not just rows of data, the Collection Assessment Team had to become more agile in using Excel to support data-driven decisions. Creating dashboards with Excel to share insights based on package evaluations, ROI assessments, and cost-per-use analysis proved to be the most expedient and cost-effective way to communicate our findings visually while also providing the underlying data within the spreadsheet. In the current landscape, stakeholders expect libraries to generate on-demand reports that explicitly underscore the data used to support decisions (Massis 2016, 131). Because a library's strategic direction and its rationale for decision making are predicated on evidence-based data (133), Excel spreadsheets remain our front-end tool for wrangling data. When working with aggregated usage data and COUNTER reports, Excel features such as Power Pivot, Power Query, and Power View, available for versions as early as 2010 and 2013, provide a customized way to glean new perspectives and insights from their data. The Collection Assessment Team began utilizing these advanced Excel options to support a more robust program of data analysis, visualization, and transparency. PivotTables, PivotCharts, and slicers are the basic tools used to create dashboards and interactive reports and allow us to provide an array of visualizations and data interactions for our stakeholders. The dashboards and visualizations that we create need to be shared in a variety of web spaces, some private and some public-facing. Using Excel on our campus Microsoft

SharePoint server allows for sharing dashboards and the underlying data in a myriad of ways.

PivotTables and PivotCharts create the basis for dynamic dashboard and visualizations. There are a number of chart options, including pie, column, bar, line, scatter, bubble, and other selections. Slicers provide a way to filter the data in a PivotChart and to dynamically change the data displayed. Essentially, slicers can act as buttons that enable quick filtering of PivotTables and PivotCharts without the need to open a drop-down list to find items, and one slicer can filter multiple PivotCharts providing various aspects of the data, which is one of the hallmarks of an effective dashboard.

The cost to acquire the software and train employees is minimal. At Virginia Tech, as for many universities and large institutions, Excel is provided via an enterprise license. Our team gained the necessary advanced skills training primarily through Lynda.com, an online learning platform that all employees can access. However, team members also utilized other free online training platforms, including the Microsoft Office 365 Training Center and YouTube. Excel's powerful analytic capabilities along with its accessibility and familiarity within the business realm make it one of the most accessible and widely used BI tools.

Redlink

Library staff are inundated with electronic resource data. Often, they spend an excessive amount of time manually downloading COUNTER and non-COUNTER usage statistics from a myriad of platforms and then consolidating the information into a single report to use in evidence-based decision making. In a survey conducted in 2014, library staff who manage electronic resources reported that an average of 40% of their time was spent collecting usage statistics (Torbert 2015, 166). In a similar survey, respondents noted that the process of gathering usage statistics takes them four weeks or longer (Welker 2012, 9). Redlink offers a remedy to this time-consuming process.

The Redlink Library Dashboard is an economical, subscription-based business intelligence tool that automates harvesting and normalizing of COUNTER and non-COUNTER usage statistics. Other stand-alone products in the market include ProQuest's Intota, EBSCO's Usage Consolidation, and Springshare's LibInsight. The Redlink Library Dashboard promises to instantly merge and organize usage and cost data into a single platform so staff can efficiently access the information on-demand. Users can quickly ascertain and evaluate relative usage of a given resource. Data can be manipulated in a number of ways at the publisher-level, discipline-level, product-level, and publication-level, as well as downloaded for further analysis into Excel. Additionally, the Library Dashboard calculates highly coveted cost-per-use metrics and produces robust data visualizations that make reading and understanding usage easier and more engaging.

The main advantages of the Redlink Library Dashboard system are:

- Saves critical staff time through the automated collection and standardization of usage statistics
- Filters and engineers data on a user-friendly, web-based, and fully hosted platform
- Reports usage and cost data on-demand for efficient sharing with staff and stakeholders
- Provides ability to compare usage and cost data for overlapping titles from multiple sources
- Creates dynamic data visualizations that expedite data analysis and decision making with more transparent, readily communicated information
- Thirty-day trials available using demo data environment (does not include a library's data)
- Online training and documentation available

A disadvantage of the Redlink Library Dashboard is:

- Significant onboarding process

A substantial time investment exists regarding the initial setup of the Redlink Library Dashboard system. Setup requires libraries to gather and send all their SUSHI protocols, login credentials, and subscription/cost information to Redlink. This "onboarding" process is estimated to take four to six weeks.

For many libraries, in-house usage collection and reporting is a preferred and viable option. Torbert (2015) describes a relevant project conducted at the University of Mississippi that evaluated the total cost of library staff gathering e-resources' usage data and creating cost-per-use reports in-house compared to outsourcing data collection and analysis using a vendor usage product, like Redlink. They compared these in-house costs to subscription price quotes for three vendor products and ultimately realized that for their library, it was still more cost-efficient to conduct these tasks internally (166). Rathmel and Currie (2015) describe their homegrown data collection and assessment process when evaluating "Big Deals" at the University of Kansas, and mention that although there are helpful vendor usage products available, none of them are the "perfect" tool (30).

The Redlink Library Dashboard is a low-cost BI tool that empowers librarians to extract meaningful information and generate compelling charts from the vast amount of electronic resource usage data, saving critical staff time and facilitating data-driven decisions. It is an efficient tool, especially for libraries that have limited staffing or do not possess the technical skills to retrieve, cleanup, and engagingly present the data. Redlink helps librarians illustrate the story of a library's usage of electronic resources, and in turn, expedites in depicting the value and impact of these costly assets.

Tableau

In addition to creating visualizations and dashboards for COUNTER usage data, the Virginia Tech team needed to work with institutional data and needed a tool that allowed for the following: sharing dynamic visualizations via the web, connecting to a wide variety of data sources, and sharing data sources among colleagues. Product reviews and word of mouth brought Virginia Tech to Tableau, a well-known BI tool particularly known for its visualizations. In 2017, *PC Magazine* named Tableau Desktop Editor's Choice Winner (Baker 2017). Users include the likes of Citibank, Toyota, Dell, and a host of universities.

At least three articles in the Association of Research Libraries' (ARL) *Research Library Issues* have highlighted the use of Tableau in academic libraries. In 2014, members at the University of British Columbia (UCB), University of Massachusetts-Amherst (UMA), and the Ohio State Universities (OSU) libraries published an article depicting Tableau's use in their assessment programs (Buhler, Lewellen, and Murphy 2016). OSU users do not specifically cite use of Tableau Public for electronic resources, but do use it to visualize reference, gate count, ARL, ILLiad, and Sierra data. Reasons for choosing Tableau included end users' ability to download and share data and visualizations. UCB utilized Tableau for data exploration of circulation statistics and a LibQual+Survey and cited Tableau's ability to quickly drill down through data as a positive factor in their use of the tool. UMA performed analysis and created dashboards for local and consortial collections, including monograph and corresponding expenditures, circulation, subject areas, and colleges. Further, they worked with consortial members to analyze and visualize a patron-driven e-book project (Buhler, Lewellen, and Murphy 2016). In the same issue of *Research Library Issues*, Lewellen and Plum (2016) detail their use of Tableau in a Mines© for Libraries study at UMA: a project exclusively focused on electronic resources. The study highlighted the ability to monitor data results in real time as a benefit. Hoffman and Hall (2017) of UNLV employ Tableau for electronic resource analysis as well as assessment, and because they also use Tableau Server they can share dashboards, visualizations, and analysis broadly throughout their library (167).

Sharing data sources works easily with Tableau Online or Tableau Server, but a strong word of caution is necessary here when it comes to most BI tools, including Tableau. To build and share visualizations and dashboards, *users need a license*. To share those dynamic visualizations and dashboards created in Tableau Desktop and the underlying data sources associated with them, users must also acquire an additional license to Tableau Online or Tableau Server, both of which present an additional cost per user. Two free alternatives exist for sharing visualizations and dashboards: Tableau Reader and Tableau Public, but both are less than ideal if your library plans to *routinely and broadly* use BI tools. Tableau Reader, which functions much like Adobe Reader, is free for anyone to download and use to view workbooks created by Tableau Desktop users. Tableau Public is an excellent choice for small projects; it ultimately limits users who need to make routine use of a BI tool. Sharing visualizations in Tableau Public means it is truly publicly available to anyone with a web browser (Tableau Server and Tableau Online require an account and sign-in). Secondly, Tableau Public limits users to 10 gigabytes of storage space. A third limitation, and a rather significant one, is that Tableau Public does not allow users to store data sources to reuse and/or share in another workbook, meaning that users may find themselves reinventing the wheel. Tableau Public also does not offer the ability to connect to as many different data sources. Lastly, Tableau Public does not offer users a way to organize and search for saved work. If your library is looking only to make a handful of publicly available visualizations via the web, Tableau Public offers users an excellent choice. Tableau Public also provides users with an embed code so that visualizations can be embedded into web pages.

Connecting to a wide variety of data source types makes BI tools very attractive. At the University of Massachusetts-Amherst Libraries, connecting to multiple data streams and "the ability to integrate and query multiple data sets also supports expectations related to campus goals, accountability, planning, and assessment" (Buhler, Lewellen, and Murphy 2016, 26). Given these criteria, UMA chose Tableau. In "Data Visualization and Rapid Analytics: Applying Tableau Desktop® to Support Library Decision-Making," the author points to the ability to blend multiple data sources as a way to "create meaningful dashboards" (Murphy 2013, 468). In addition to working with data collected in Excel or CSV files, Tableau users can connect to a number of file types and servers, including Excel, JSON, Microsoft Access, statistical files, Google Sheets, SAP, Snowflake, MySQL, multiple Amazon services, Dropbox, Microsoft SQL Server, and web data connectors. The latter provides a way to connect to social media resources like Facebook and Twitter. Our experience at this time is limited to connecting Excel, CSV, Google Sheets, Google Analytics, and gate count software. Connecting to the first four were extremely simple, while the latter presented more difficulties because of problems with the gate count software.

Given the ability to connect to so many data sources, several uses of Tableau currently exist and plans are under way for other projects. The first use involves ARL, National Center for Education Statistics (NCES), and institutional data. Tableau made it relatively easy to blend these CSV data sources by institution name using the join, union, and blending functions, all of which operate as SQL does. In this case, administrators often found themselves requesting the same type visualizations but with caveats or an additional calculation. Tableau allowed Virginia Tech to connect to those data sources, blend them, and build dashboards that allow end users to change views on the fly using drop-down boxes and highlighters. Further, one visualization can be used to filter multiple visualizations on the same page. Secondly, like Excel, Tableau allows users to create formulas. In this case, Virginia Tech used existing ARL data but normalized it to account for student body size. To do so, the dashboard creator simply had to create a calculation using existing data, which creates an additional field but does not change underlying data.

Virginia Tech also currently employs Tableau to review its subscription with all Elsevier content. In this case, the dashboard creator pulled together separate CSV files containing COUNTER usage data (JR1 and JR5), subscription-type information (consortial, individual), resource type (e-books and journals), and cost data. The dashboards allow end users to filter by resource type and subscription type. Parameters can be set to show subsets, like a Top 100 titles used or titles with a cost-per-use within a specific percentage range. Views of usage can be quickly manipulated to show calendar year, fiscal year, or monthly totals. Tools like "Quick Calculations" allow users to compute percentages of data, such as computing the percentage of particular journal title's usage to the overall usage of all Elsevier titles. The "analytics" tool provides a way with just one click to show average and median lines with or without confidence intervals, distribution bands, trend lines, forecasts, box plots, and cluster charts. Using similar dashboards, Virginia Tech has connected directly to gate count software to display patron movement in and out of exits; connection to that software was relatively simple, but the gate count software itself is problematic. Lastly, plans exist to connect to a newly implemented Integrated Library System (ILS) and as well as card swipe technologies used by patrons using specialized labs and spaces within the library.

The Oneonta Project

The following case will demonstrate how a business intelligence project looks like in real life. Today, most academic libraries are spending a significant amount of money on electronic resources. In 2016, North American academic libraries spent 70% of their materials expenditure budget on electronic resources (PCG 2017). While many vendors increase the subscription cost of their products every year, most libraries will not receive a budget increase. According to the Public Communications Group (PCG) *Library Budget Predictions for 2017*, 49% of North American libraries' budgets will remain static, 25% will experience a budget cut, and only 23% will receive a budget increase.

These unfortunate circumstances require libraries to maintain meticulous and careful optimization of their financial resources to satisfy information demands from patrons. Therefore, for budget optimization, it will be helpful if librarians possess a clear statistical view of the trends and patterns in price changes. Visualized data will also help to support decision making in the library, or for communicating information to the university administration.

Finally, since statistics analysis and data visualization have been proven to be an efficient tool to help libraries manage their assets, including but not limited to electronic resources, it will be helpful for smaller libraries to practice methodology and techniques for such operations.

Increasingly, libraries are applying statistical analysis and data visualization to help them better assess and manage their electronic resources. For example, librarians from the Yale University Libraries developed measurements to evaluate the performance of their Ebrary/ProQuest e-book packages by measuring the difference between the proportion of total usage and the proportion of titles in the entire collection (Linden, Sidman, and Tudesco 2015). Other practices include research at the Pennsylvania State University, University Park, to use web analytics to develop the foundational framework to evaluate electronic journals by comparing the usage and cost in each founding group (Coughlin, Campbell, and Jansen 2016). Since these practices were widely accepted and practiced in different academic libraries, librarians from different SUNY institutions conducted a research project targeting price changing trends of electronic resources through statistics and data visualization.

According to a 2018 article (Skerrett), Netflix has three rules for data analysis: (1) data should be accessible, easy to discover, and easy to process for everyone; (2) no matter what the size of the dataset, the data visualization is critical for understanding; and (3) hard-to-find data are less valuable. Following these three rules, after the data cleanup, more than 80 aggregating databases with consistent payment records from 2010 to 2015 were selected for the project, and their payment records, as well as their usage data, were extracted from the ILS and administrative platforms. To keep all data consistent and relative, no electronic serials, one-time purchases, or annual access fees were included. A student intern from the Department of Statistics at SUNY Oneonta was hired to process the data, and the intern used Excel and IBM SPSS for statistical analysis and data visualization. After input of cleaned payment expenditure data from the ILS into Excel, graphs of the average and median cost of selected titles, as well as the percentage increase over the years were created. The visualized data indicate a consistent price increase since 2011, and the price increases in 2014 and 2015 were fierce.

IBM SPSS was used to compare prices and usage of selected resources and to predict future price changes, which was evaluated by their correlation to existing expenditure statistics from 2010 to 2015. The visualized data suggest resources with higher usage tend to cost more, probably because to vendors high usage indicates high demand. Meanwhile, the projections suggest that in 2017 and 2018 the price change may be relatively moderate, which is likely a sign that this price increase cycle is approaching its cap. It is important to note that the model for future price prediction is based on the expenditure data from the previous years, and that value varies based on vendor. Therefore, the further into the future the prediction, the less accurate it is. It is also important to note that compared to the enormous size of the aggregating databases market with numerous products available, this project covered only a very small segment.

Through the visualized data, it is evident that the pricing trend has been influenced by the national economic trend—the high percentage of price increase during 2014/2015 correlated to the steep value increase of the U.S. dollar in the same period, and the relatively moderate price increase of electronic resources since 2015 could also be related to the relatively moderate value change of the U.S. dollar. However, most major vendors do not publish detailed revenue reports since they are privately owned. Hence, there is a lack of information to determine the causes of price changes other than the national economic picture and the product demand.

In conclusion, this project provided a visualized trend of electronic resources price changes, as well as a prediction of future prices. It also offered an opportunity to practice data visualization and statistical analysis in small academic libraries without any additional cost. Overall, this project was a very beneficial exercise and provided a view of the price changing trends of electronic resources.

SUMMARY

Statistical analysis and data visualization are critical when communicating vision and decision data to administration and stakeholders. Increasingly, libraries will turn to a BI tool to assist with the analyzing and communicating insights about their data. Each library, however, presents unique situations, especially regarding how much an institution can invest in such a tool, but also in the demand for the number of visualizations, dashboards, and reports needed. Of the BI tools reviewed here, Tableau offers a better product if an institution desires a tool that can handle virtually any need and present sophisticated visualizations—but it comes at the highest cost. If institutions seek a tool just for electronic resources, Redlink offers an excellent choice. Excel provides a strong middle ground approach. It can handle a wide variety of data types, execute sophisticated calculations, and deliver aesthetically pleasing visualizations better than ever. Its significant drawback rests in its lack of a convenient, cloud-based sharing mechanism, yet Excel still provides substantial benefits to its users.

WORKS CITED

Baker, Pam. 2017. "BARC Survey: Data Discovery and Self-Service BI Tools Remain Dominant User Trends." *Wireless News. InfoTrac Computer Database*, EBSCO*host* (accessed July 13, 2018).

Baker, Pam. 2017. "The Best Self-Service Business Intelligence (BI) Tools of 2017." *PC Magazine*. May 26. http://www.pcmag.com/article2/0,2817,2491954,00.asp.

Bosch, Stephen, Barbara Albee, and Kittie Henderson. 2018. "Death by 1,000 Cuts: Flat Budgets, Price Increases, and a Reliance on Status Journals for Tenure and Promotion Keep Familiar Pressures on the Serials Marketplace." *Library Journal* 28. *Literature Resource Center*, EBSCO*host* (accessed April 15, 2018).

Buhler, Jeremy, Rachel Lewellen, and Sarah Anne Murphy. 2016. "Tableau Unleashed: Visualizing Library Data." *Research Library Issues* 288: 21–36. *Library Literature & Information Science Full Text (H.W. Wilson)*, EBSCO*host* (accessed March 3, 2018).

Chen, Hsuanwei Michelle. 2017. "An Overview of Information Visualization." *Library Technology Reports* 53(3): 5–7.

Coughlin, Daniel M., Mark C. Campbell, and Bernard J. Jansen. 2016. "A Web Analytics Approach for Appraising Electronic Resources in Academic Libraries." *Journal of the Association for Information Science & Technology* 67(3): 518–534. *Business Source Complete*, EBSCO*host* (accessed July 13, 2018).

Hoffman, Starr, and Ashley Hall. 2017. "The Data Framework: A Collaborative Tool for Assessment at the UNLV Libraries." *Journal of Electronic Resources Librarianship* 29(3): 159–167. *Library, Information Science & Technology Abstracts*, EBSCO*host* (accessed April 7, 2018).

Kilb, Megan, and Matt Jansen. 2016. "Visualizing Collections Data: Why Pie Charts Aren't Always the Answer." *Serials Review* 42(3): 192–200. *Academic Search Complete*, EBSCO*host* (accessed April 7, 2018).

Lewellen, Rachel, and Terry Plum. 2016. "Assessment of E-Resource Usage at University of Massachusetts Amherst: A MINES for Libraries® Study Using Tableau for Visualization and Analysis." *Research Library Issues* 288: 5–20. *Library Literature & Information Science Full Text (H.W. Wilson)*, EBSCO*host* (accessed July 13, 2018).

Linden, Julie, Angela Sidman, and Sarah Tudesco. "Ebrary on the Radar." *ACRL 2015 Proceedings*. March 2015. http://www.ala.org/acrl/sites/ala.org.acrl/files/content/conferences/confsandpreconfs/2015/Linden_Sidman_Tudesco.pdf

Magnuson, Lauren, ed. 2016. *Data Visualization: A Guide to Visual Storytelling for Libraries*. Lanham, MD: Rowman & Littlefield.

Massis, Bruce. 2016. "Data-Driven Decision-Making in the Library." *New Library World* 117(1/2): 131–134. doi:10.1108/NLW-10-2015-0081

Murphy, Sarah Anne. 2013. "Data Visualization and Rapid Analytics: Applying Tableau Desktop to Support Library Decision-Making." *Journal of Web Librarianship* 7(4): 465–476. *Library, Information Science & Technology Abstracts*, EBSCO*host* (accessed April 7, 2018).

Powell, Allen. 2011. "Times of Crisis Accelerate Inevitable Change." *Journal of Library Administration* 51(1): 105–129. *Education Research Complete*, EBSCO*host* (accessed May 13, 2018).

Public Communications Group (PCG). 2017. "Library Budget Predictions for 2017." http://www.pcgplus.com/wp-content/uploads/2017/05/Library-Budget-Predictions-for-2017-public.pdf

Rathmel, Angie, Lea Currie, and Todd Enoch. 2015. ""Big Deals" and Squeaky Wheels: Taking Stock of Your Stats." *Serials Librarian* 68 (1–4): 26–37. *Library Literature & Information Science Full Text (H. W. Wilson)*, EBSCO*host* (accessed May 13, 2018).

Skerrett, David. 2018. "Why Data Is the New Oil." *EContent* Spring 2018. http://www.econtentmag.com/Articles/Editorial/Mobile-Moment/Why-Data-Is-the-New-Oil-124552.htm

Torbert, Christina. 2015. "Cost-per-Use versus Hours-per-Report: Usage Reporting and the Value of Staff Time." *Serials Librarian* 68(1–4): 163–167. *Library Literature & Information Science Full Text (H. W. Wilson)*, EBSCO*host* (accessed May 7, 2018).

Welker, Josh. 2012. "Counting on COUNTER: The Current State of e-Resource Usage Data in Libraries." *Computers in Libraries* 32(9): 6–12. *Business Insights Global*, EBSCO*host* (accessed June 1, 2018).

Additional Reading

Ali, Syed Mohd, Noopur Gupta Nayak, Krishna Gopal, and Rakesh Kumar Lenka. 2016. "Big Data Visualization: Tools and Challenges." *2016 2nd International Conference on Contemporary Computing and Informatics (IC3I)*. doi:10.1109/IC3I.2016.7918044

Kyrillidou, Martha. 2016. "Business Intelligence and Data Visualization with Tableau in Research Libraries." *Research Library Issues* no. 288: 1–4. *Library Literature & Information Science Full Text (H. W. Wilson)*, EBSCO*host* (accessed May 5, 2018).

Lougen, Colleen. 2017. "Redlink." *Charleston Advisor* 19(2): 55–59.

Miller, Andrea. 2014. "Application of Excel® Pivot Tables and Pivot Charts for Efficient Library Data Analysis and Illustration." *Journal of Library Administration* 54 (3): 169–186.*Education Research Complete*, EBSCO*host* (accessed July 13, 2018).

Miller, Andrea. 2014. "Introduction to Using Excel Pivot Tables and Pivot Charts to Increase Efficiency in Library Data Analysis and Illustration." *Journal of Library Administration* 54(2): 94–106. *Education Research Complete*, EBSCO*host* (accessed June 10, 2018).

Murphy, Sarah Anne. 2015. "How Data Visualization Supports Academic Library Assessment." *College & Research Libraries News* 76(9): 482–486. *Library Literature & Information Science Full Text (H. W. Wilson)*, EBSCO*host* (accessed April 11, 2018).

Tattersall, Andy, and Maria J. Grant. 2016. "Big Data—What Is It and Why It Matters." *Health Information & Libraries Journal* June: 89–91. *Academic Search Complete*, EBSCO*host* (accessed April 20, 2018).

Tront, Russell, and Suzanne Hoffman. 2011. "Pervasive Business Intelligence and the Realities of Excel." *Business Intelligence Journal* 16(4): 8–14. *Business Source Complete*, EBSCO*host* (accessed March 1, 2018).

IMPACT ANALYTICS: EMPOWERING LIBRARIES TO EVALUATE THE MEANINGFUL USE OF E-RESOURCES

Helen Adey
Resource Acquisitions & Supply Team Manager,
Libraries & Learning Resource, Nottingham Trent
University, helen.adey@ntu.ac.uk

Jesse Koennecke
Director, Acquisitions & E-Resource Licensing Services,
Cornell University, jtk1@cornell.edu

Andrea Eastman-Mullins
Vice President Product Management, Alexander Street,
a ProQuest Company, aeastmanmullins@astreetpress.com

ABSTRACT

Data is easy, but insight is hard. With COUNTER, Google Analytics, and user engagement reports, we have more data than ever on how e-resources are used. While the first step is making this data available, the next step is determining how these analytics can empower the library to evaluate true educational and research impact. The next frontier requires collaboration between publishers and librarians. In this chapter, Helen Adey (Nottingham Trent University), Jesse Koennecke (Cornell University), and Andrea Eastman-Mullins (Alexander Street) describe the different approaches being adopted at Cornell, Nottingham Trent, and Alexander Street to go beyond simple analysis of usage, to impact and engagement metrics, which can support effective decision making.

INTRODUCTION

For many years, libraries and publishers have considered usage statistics to be core metrics in decision making. Items that have low use are often relegated or discarded, and the inclusion of cost-per-use data in serials renewal decision making has become commonplace.

However, usage data on its own actually gives libraries and publishers very little insight into how content is being used or how much it is being looked at—and libraries are becoming increasingly interested in metrics that may give an indication of how resources are being used and the extent to which library users value the resources they provide.

The introduction of less-traditional digital content, in the form of multimedia and primary digital sources, has led to the development and production of new types of analytical data with the goal of demonstrating both user engagement and the impact of use. As library collection budgets fall under more pressure, and the need to demonstrate value for money in higher education increases, libraries are turning to data and analytics to provide both evidence and insight. However, not all libraries will have the capacity, resources, and expertise required to carry out in-depth analyses, and the current lack of any agreed-upon data standards means that both libraries and publishers are still experimenting with what might be possible in terms of analytics and the conclusions be drawn from them.

This chapter shares some early experiences, experiments, and perspectives from both publishers and universities in the United States and the United Kingdom. It aims to demonstrate how new types of analytics can go beyond simple cost-per-use calculations to support effective decision making and suggests ways in which these analytics can improve librarians' understanding of how library users are engaging with the resources they provide.

NOTTINGHAM TRENT UNIVERSITY CASE STUDY

Staff in the Nottingham Trent University (NTU)'s Libraries & Learning Resources (LLR) department have been collecting and monitoring usage statistics compliant with Counting Online Usage of Networked Electronic Resources (COUNTER) for many years, using them to help inform and underpin decision making. These core metrics drive electronic serials and database renewal decisions, have provided evidence to support cancellation decisions, and have triggered acquisitions when presented in the form of turnaway and access-denial statistics. In short, they have become an everyday part of managing electronic resources. As library collections move away from print and become increasingly electronic, usage becomes less visible and more anonymous, making usage statistics the only real evidence and indication of how well libraries are fulfilling the needs of their customers. LLR staff also have wide experience in using multiple evidence-based acquisition (EBA) plans, where analysis of usage is an integral part of the final decisions on which content to purchase in perpetuity. These early experiments proved that there are often significant challenges to be faced when analyzing and understanding the data from different publisher plans.

Evidence-Based Acquisition

In 2015, LLR launched a service called Your Books More Books (YBMB) in an effort to supply undergraduates and postgraduates with any items that were not already in stock—and fulfill these requests within three days. The library was trying to find a solution for the unpredictable information needs of students completing their final year dissertations and postgraduate theses. We launched five EBA plans from major publishers with the goal of significantly increasing the number of e-books available to these users.

As part of the final decision making on which EBA content the library should retain at the end of the plans, the publishers provided the library with conventional COUNTER usage statistics. These showed that each plan had been used differently, and the funds deposited at the start of the plan had performed in wildly different ways. For example, the funds deposited in one plan could purchase all items used seven times or more; with another plan, the funds were only able to purchase items used nine times or more; the third plan, 25 times or more. Because this was the library's first experience with EBA plans, we were uncertain about whether these inconsistencies were a cause for concern, and we were aware that there was no common understanding or agreement on what would constitute "good" usage.

These doubts and experiences were the primary impetus for the library staff to consider and question what sort of metrics and data *would* be helpful when trying to make decisions about the way our customers value our collections, and how they might be supporting their learning and research needs. In particular, we questioned the following:

- Is the duration or time spent in using a resource more meaningful than the number of times an item has been viewed?
- What other types of measurable usage might be meaningful and provide us with better evidence on which to base our acquisition decision making and service delivery?

LLR had also started to experiment with other types of digital content, including an EBA plan from Alexander Street, a ProQuest Company, that included a range of multimedia resources. At the end of the license period for the plan, library staff made the selection of which Alexander Street content was to be retained in perpetuity by using only conventional COUNTER usage statistics. We used the COUNTER data and title prices to establish which titles could be acquired using the deposited funds and found that with the Alexander Street EBA plan, the available funds ran out part way through a group of resources that had all received the same number of uses. The absence of any other metric on which to base our decision making provided the impetus for NTU LLR and Alexander Street to collaborate on developing a suite of user engagement analytics for use in EBA decision-making processes.

Findings

Throughout the process of developing and testing the new data, it quickly became clear that the new engagement analytics being developed by Alexander Street were both fascinating and useful in not only the decision-making processes that arise at the end of an EBA plan, but they also had the potential to inform other decision-making activities.

Unsurprisingly, both the quality and range of data from the user engagement analytics were far richer than we were finding with COUNTER usage reports.

Having concluded an EBA plan with Alexander Street, LLR now has experience with using these engagement metrics in practice, and it has influenced some of our decisions. The majority of the content chosen for retention at the end of the plan was still the content that had received the highest use, but there were some instances of content being selected where a greater percentage of the

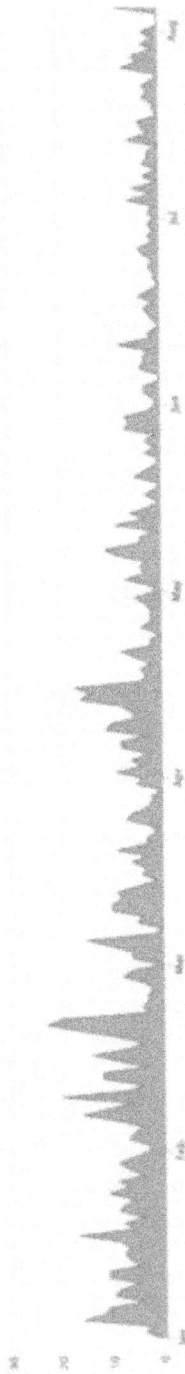

TITLE   SUBJECT AREA   PUBLISHER   COLLECTION

Title	Average % Played	Total	JAN 2017	FEB 2017	MAR 2017	APR 2017	MAY 2017	JUN 2017	JUL 2017	AUG 2017
Free Schools	41.91%	16	0	15	0	1	0	0	0	0
Social Media	3.61%	16	1	0	0	0	0	1	1	13
Foundations	26.65%	12	2	8	0	0	1	0	1	0
House 2006	17.73%	11	0	2	0	2	6	0	1	0
Assessment for Learning	45.20%	7	0	0	0	1	0	0	6	0
Corporate Social Responsibility	0.54%	7	1	3	1	2	0	0	0	0
Roof Structure	74.92%	7	1	4	0	0	2	0	0	0
The New Academies	14.04%	7	0	0	7	0	0	0	0	0
Ground Floors	29.42%	7	1	5	0	0	1	0	0	0
Strategy and Research Methods Development	0.15%	6	3	1	2	0	0	0	0	0

Load More

PlayBack   Engagement   Accessibility   Patron

Alexander Street Title Usage Chart

resource had been watched, as opposed to other resources that had received more views but a smaller percentage of the content had been viewed.

The figure that follows contains conventional usage data showing the most used items in descending order, but it also shows on average how much of the content was played. It is interesting to see here that the item with the largest average percentage played is *not* the most-viewed title.

These analytics proved to be very helpful when fine-tuning the library's selections. LLR's experience of EBA plans indicates that rarely do deposited EBA funds run out at the exact same point that all content with the same amount of usage can be selected for retention. In the absence of any other data such as engagement analytics, this means libraries will usually be required to choose between different titles that have all received the same amount of usage in COUNTER metric terms.

At the end of the Alexander Street EBA plan, LLR was able to see some resources had been viewed the same number of times, but the average percentage played differed from title to title, and ultimately, this proved to be their deciding factor.

Insights into User Behaviors

Overall, LLR's experience of using the engagement analytics reporting has confirmed our belief that they add both value and insight into user behavior.

For instance, when analytics show that users have cited an item, this strongly suggests that a user feels the content has both importance and value. The same can be said for metrics demonstrating that content has been shared, added to a playlist, watched on a mobile device, e-mailed, or saved. LLR feels that all these metrics have the potential to offer useful insight beyond merely influencing decisions that affect acquisitions.

Value as a Marketing Tool

Marketing and promotion of resources are becoming more important to libraries, and the granularity of the Alexander Street data gives libraries the chance to try out different marketing tools and routes, and to watch for an impact in the user engagement analytics. This is an area of work that NTU library staff wish to explore in the coming months, once we have identified robust sampling techniques. For example, what is most effective—Facebook, Twitter, or word of mouth? Finding the answer to this question in the data will be critical in informing decision making for marketing campaigns and other activities.

Next Steps

The additional insights gained from the user engagement analytics have already proved valuable, and LLR would like to make greater use of the data in the future.

We do, however, recognize that while the temptation to try to find out more about what our customers like and value is almost overwhelming, there is a possible tension between this desire and seamless and non-intrusive access to content.

The interactive nature of Alexander Street's platform, where users can rate videos or provide information about how content has been used, also raises questions regarding whether libraries can trust users to be honest in their responses. For example, if data shows an opera has been watched at an institution with no music or creative arts courses, might this use have been for recreational or entertainment purposes, and would the user admit this, or would they select a more academic reason?

We also believe that that more work is needed to understand how to interpret "low percentage played" data—libraries don't expect users to start reading all e-books at page one and continue to the end, so what would be the engagement markers of good targeted usage of resources, as opposed to the randomness of dipping in and out?

LLR would also like to explore the idea of engagement analytics for text-based materials, which make up the majority of our collection. We know not all e-book and e-journal platforms have the same level of interactivity as video-based platforms, but LLR would like to see more traditional forms of publishing starting to include data beyond simple usage.

The fact that most e-book and e-journal platforms can detect how much content has been printed or copied suggests that it should be possible to at least report on how much content has been used. LLR staff would welcome the opportunity to work collaboratively with other vendors and content providers to explore the opportunities and benefits of increased evidence, data, and analytics on which to base our collection decisions and drive service developments.

Helen Adey
ORCID ID: http://orcid.org/ 0000-0001-6173-8744

CORNELL UNIVERSITY LIBRARY (CUL) CASE STUDY

As we explore the concept of impact analytics and how we can look beyond COUNTER usage to get a better picture of the value a resource brings to the institution and its users, it is possible to see how these concepts can be applied to other types of content. Electronic journals, for example, constitute a significant portion of what many academic libraries spend their collection funds on every year, and as budgets tighten, it becomes increasingly important to strategically review these subscriptions and package deals to ensure we are focusing on the most important resources.

At CUL, we have been looking at ways to go beyond cost-per-use analysis and to introduce the concepts of impact or engagement analytics into our e-journal renewal review process. We realize that not all uses are equal and that a title that might not be highly used may be just as important, or even more so, than one that sees considerable use. To try to get a clearer picture of this, staff at CUL have engaged in several projects recently to try to evaluate the impact these journals have on our users.

Through these steps we have identified several factors or types of data that might be useful for evaluating impact. Some of these are used routinely by libraries to review their e-journal subscriptions. On their own, each of these factors can tell us something about the value or impact a title may bring to our users but may not give a complete picture. By combining some of these, we can start to see how the data can help in our decision making even when confronted with ambiguity. The types of data we have considered in our recent efforts include:

- *Usage:* From a count of uses and turnaways we can readily get from publishers and information providers' COUNTER reports, we can compare some relative value across a list of journals, we can try to understand trends over time, and we can spot peaks that might indicate a targeted interest such as use in a course. Usage has long been considered an indicator of importance for a journal at many institutions, but it typically lacks any way to understand the real impact the journal has on scholarship.
- *Cost:* Libraries may consider several different cost points while evaluating the value of a journal. We can typically obtain a list price, but we might actually pay a different amount—perhaps we call that our price. We can derive a package price for a title out of a collection of

titles paid together. Each of these could be useful in helping us understand the cost per use or compare the arrangements we have with the publishers. These different prices may all come from different sources—serials vendors, directly from the publisher, our acquisitions systems, or derived from other data.

- *Journal quality measures: Impact Factor* (Clarivate Analytics/Web of Knowledge), *CiteScore* (Elsevier/Scopus), and other external measures can be used to weigh journals across a discipline or help in some renewal decision making. However, these measures do not take into account the impact a journal may have for the individual or the institution.
- *Institutional factors:* Articles cited or written by members of our institution might help us understand the quality of use or the impact a journal brings to our own community.

In discussions about journal renewals and cancellations at Cornell, we have typically been able to bring the cost and use data we have available together effectively to produce a cost-per-use list that we can review. Like many other libraries, we have accomplished this to varying degrees of success with spreadsheets, electronic records management systems, and custom databases. The Excel VLOOKUP and similar functions can bring together different data sources and have been used for cost-per-use analysis for many years.

Most of the time, these lists can be broken down into three categories:

- *High-use/low cost-per-use titles* that we assume bring some value to our users and may not need to review further.
- *Little to no use or a considerably high cost-per-use* that we might consider for cancellation. We may want to bring in further data about these journals before making a final decision, such as how new the title is, or recently expressed interest from a department or other group of users.
- *Titles with middling total use or an above-average cost-per-use.* This is the list that often requires the most work to review, particularly in tighter budget years. How important are these titles to our users or to some part of our collection and is there a way to use data to help us get a clearer understanding of the local impact of the title? Can we provide our subject librarians with data that can help them reduce the time they might need to spend on journal renewal and cancellation decisions?

By combining additional sources of data, we can try to add a quantitative element to what has traditionally been a qualitative process. When we hear that a title is important to a field, is there evidence to support that or to show that it is important to our specific users? Bringing in other data sources, we might be able to confirm or refute some of this anecdotal information.

For example, if we value titles that our faculty frequently refer to or publish in, we could bring in author affiliation or citation data from Scopus or Web of Science. Combining this data with COUNTER usage, we could see something what is shown in the chart that follows.

Chart 1: Sample Comparison–Journal Usage versus Author Affiliation

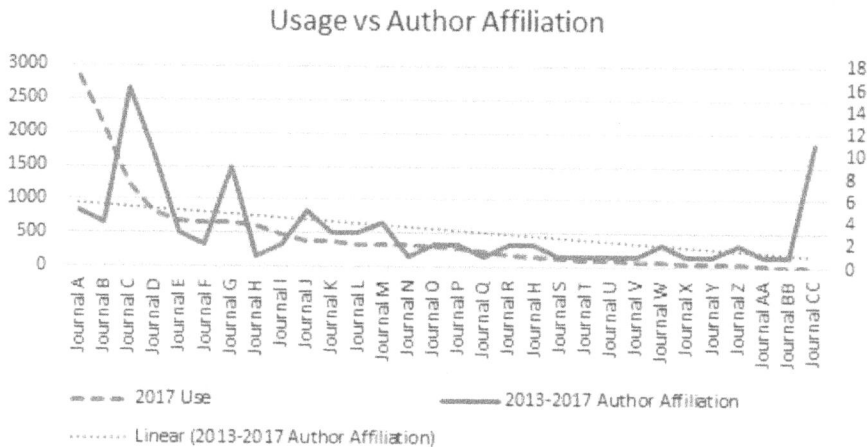

Usage vs Author Affiliation

In the chart, we see the 2017 usage data for 29 journals charted along with the number of articles published between 2013 and 2017 in those journals with at least one Cornell University–affiliated author (from Scopus).

This chart raises a few questions:

- Journal CC shows zero usage, but 11 affiliated articles. This seems likely to be a data mismatch. In any case, further investigation is needed before targeting this journal for cancellation based on its lack of use.

- The linear trendline for author affiliation tracks somewhat with the usage metric. Does it make sense that these two metrics typically would track along a similar pattern?

- Finally, several journals in the sample show a peak in author affiliation that falls above the trendline and above the usage line. Depending on the usage threshold being considered for cancellation, these titles could be important to look at more closely.

This kind of data merging can be done with tools like Excel. However, it can be time consuming, particularly if it has to be redone each year, or for different lists of titles. We have continued to explore both what data is most useful for demonstrating impact for our users and how we might systematically pull this data together.

Student Project

In the fall 2017 semester, we engaged with a Cornell professor who was looking for projects for a business intelligence systems course he was teaching. The project we settled on was to provide multiple data sources related to several of the large journal publishers with which we hold subscriptions and big-deal packages.

We provided the following data to the student teams:

- *Title lists* from three major publishers, in different formats, covering approximately 4,000 journals
- *Usage:* A combined COUNTER-based report from our Intota Assessment system covering the same group of publishers
- *Cost (list price) from the publisher's title lists* or as an additional data set
- *Cost (our price)—Cornell's cost* pulled from renewal price lists or derived from a package total cost
- *Cornell author affiliations*—last five years of article-level data exported from Scopus
- *Access issues* as reported by our Callisto system (Sharp Moon Inc.)—this includes reports of platform downtime

Over the course of the project, we met with the class several times to answer their questions and help them understand the data. Although the course was too short to produce usable final products, the student groups did present the results of their data analysis and proposed some visualization ideas that they thought might help us in our decision making. The key things we learned during this project were:

Our data can be understood: It took some time, but with relatively few interactions with us, these students who had no prior experience with journal data developed relevant data models and could see the interconnections between the data elements. Essentially, the learning curve to understand our data was not as significant a challenge as we expected.

ISSNs are not an ideal match point: In many cases, the students experienced problems matching the data elements from one data source to another. We may not have a better way than ISSN to match journal title data from different sources, but it is a far from perfect fit. Each data source typically included one or more ISSNs but did not reliably use a common one. We need a reliable way to disambiguate ISSNs or titles to get the most out this data.

Our data is messy: some of the data, particularly title and price lists from vendors, came in different forms ranging from Excel files to PDFs. Each of these was formatted differently and included different, possibly relevant data elements. Although the students found ways to work with each different format, it poses a significant problem in the future if we want to automate gathering and integrating the appropriate data sources.

Next Steps

We recently engaged with a Cornell ontologist and developer to explore integrating this data into a more user-friendly dashboard. Although this project is in its early stages, we have been able to use much of what we learned already to get a strong start. The ontologist has met with us and other relevant staff and reviewed data sources to develop a visual model of how e-journal data interconnects. At each stage, the model is evolving to become a framework for the developer—who specializes in user interfaces and workflow—to turn into a set of tools or dashboard. We will do additional work to normalize data and minimize data matching problems. The primary users of this will be collection development librarians as they consider their journal subscriptions, work with the faculty and students they represent, and make short- and long-term financial decisions for the collection.

Jesse Koennecke

ORCHID ID: https://orcid.org/0000-0003-4047-6735

PUBLISHER PERSPECTIVE

As libraries move more toward evidence-based acquisition, publishers like Alexander Street have a role to play in offering demand-driven models and tools to help libraries better understand the impact of use. For libraries to move beyond a cost-per-use analysis, publishers must be more transparent about their usage of electronic resources, including books, journals, and multimedia. Project COUNTER remains essential for comparing frequency of use across all vendor databases, as it provides the only standard definition of usage that all vendors must follow. This data helps libraries isolate high- and low-use content, but better tools are needed to make informed decisions about all the use in between.

To support demand-driven models, publishers have gone a step further to supply item-level usage to show which titles, publishers, and subjects are being used. But even this data is not revealing what the user does with the content beyond viewing it. Was the search a new discovery or a dead end? Was the video shown in a lecture hall of more than 100 students, or viewed on a mobile device for entertainment? Was the short duration of play due to lack of interest— or was it an annotated clip assigned for class? By exposing more data on user behavior, vendors can help libraries identify when use is low but still significant.

In 2017, Alexander Street made these and other data available via a user engagement portal (see Figure 1), and piloted the data with libraries like NTU and Cornell to determine which data were most valuable.

Alexander Street's portal shares over 50 categories of data on usage. At launch, it reported the use of streaming video and, in 2018, includes streaming audio. Based on feedback, it may expand to text-based primary source formats in the future. The portal shares:

- *Playbacks:* the number of times a video or audio track was played by title, subject, collection, and publisher, including average duration of playback.

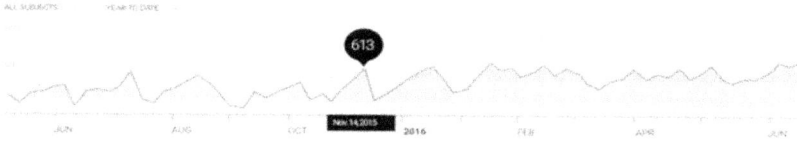

Usage Statistics by Titles

ALL SUBJECTS   YEAR TO DATE

613

Nov 14, 2015

JUN   AUG   OCT   2016   FEB   APR   JUN

Top 5: Playbacks by Subject Areas   Total Views   51353

Dance   Counseling & Therapy   American History   Anthropology   Women's Studies   All Other

Top 5: Playbacks by Collections   Total Views   51353

VAST: Academic Video Online   Dance in Video, Volume 1   Academic Video Online: Premium
Counseling and Therapy in Video, Volume 1   Filmakers Library Online, Volume 1   All Other

Dance in Videos   31%

At A Glance

Visitor Trends   1234   ASP Global 1234567

Page Views   1234   ASP Global 12345678

Subject Area Playbacks   Subjects 5   Total 1234   ASP Global 12345678

Shared 123

Cited 123

Titles Playbacks   1234   ASP Global 12345678

Extracted 123

Multimedia Playbacks Duration   42

Uploads   123   1032   02   876

Playlists 123

Title Report	Patron Reports	Accessibility Reports	Engagement Reports
Title Report	Browses Used	Transcripts Played	Cited Items
Subjects	Devices	Subtitles Played	Shared
IP/Publisher	ON/OFF Campus	On Screen Transcript Played	Sent to Mobile
Title Previewed	Days of the Week	JAWS used	Playlists Created
Playback Duration	Hours of the day		Annotations / Bookmarks
# of pageviews	Referral URLs		Browses Used
			Uploads
			Most Used Search Term
			Duration of Visit

- *Preview playbacks:* all views of 30-second previews of videos for which the library does not provide access. Campus use of these previews by title, subject, collection, and publisher is shared with the library to assist in collection development.
- *Patron reports:* information about the user population, including mobile access, operating systems, busiest times of day, referring URLs, and so on.
- *Accessibility reports:* how many times accessible features were used—including synchronous scrolling transcripts, subtitles, and on-screen transcription.
- *Engagement reports:* measure additional interaction with a title other than just a playback. For example, Alexander Street tracks if the title was annotated, saved to a playlist, embedded, shared, cited, and so on. It also captures curated views, which are views from a link that was shared by others via an LMS embed, social media post, or other citation.
- *Impact reports:* these reports capture a deeper story about use. The portal collects user feedback and reports how the video was used (assignment, shown in class, for entertainment, for research, etc.) and what rating the user gave the video. In the future it will cover metrics demonstrating learning outcomes via video interactions. Alexander Street is partnering now with faculty and libraries to measure and report on video interaction and quizzing. Aggregate results from these interactions would be shared with the library, and individual student responses shared with faculty via the LMS (see Figure 2).

Publisher Challenges and Opportunities

Along with Alexander Street, other publishers are experimenting with engagement analytics to help libraries evaluate a variety of content. Yet with no-agreed definitions or standards in engagement analytics, each vendor must make individual decisions on how to calculate this use. For example:

- Alexander Street's operas and other performances are indexed at the movement or scene level. When a user plays three movements of the same opera on separate occasions, that counts as three playbacks of the opera. If the movements are played sequentially, does the same logic apply? The decision was taken to count the parent-level playback only—so three movements equal one playback of the opera. But this

Engagement

EARLIER   1D   1W   1M   3M   1Y   ALL   CUSTOM   LATER

Title Engagement

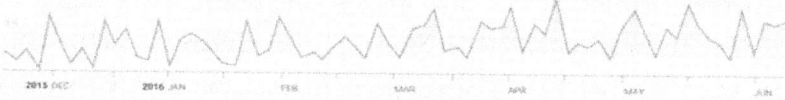

2015 DEC   2016 JAN   FEB   MAR   APR   MAY   JUN

CITED	183	SHARED	2,348	MOBILE PLAYBACK	830
PLAYLISTS	328	CLIPS	248	EMBEDS	328
CURATED VIEWS	328	EXTRACTED	123		

Impact Reports

USE CASE

6 Use Cases

Shown in class	123
Assigned to view outside of class	78
Research project	34
Entertainment	21
Training & Continuing Education	13
Other write in	134

RATED VIDEOS 248

VIDEO INTERACTIONS

Top Titles

Buying & Selling: How Trading	123
The Invisible Hand: An Introd.	78
Manners At Work	34
Basic Oxygen Administration	21
Basic Influencing Skills, 4th Ed.	13

ALEXANDER STREET

Playback: Playback by Titles, Playback by Subject Area, Playback by Publishers, Playback by Collections, Playback by Sample / Preview Content

Engagement: Cited, Shared, Mobile Playback, Uploads, Playlists, Clips, Embeds, Curated Views, Use Cases, Rated Videos, Video Interactions

Accessibility: Transcripts Played, Onscreen Subtitles / Transcripts Played

Patron: Browsers, Devices, Operating Systems, On/Off Campus, Time of the day/week decision could vary from one publisher to the other and therefore impact evaluation and even acquisition of the video.

- Reporting on user engagement requires that the software platform provide tools to engage the user. Variations in these features from platform to platform can limit what is comparable about engagement. For example, on Alexander Street's platform, users can isolate sections of a video and make a clip or playlist, which can then be shared with other users. Engagement analytics track how many times clips and playlists are created and viewed. Across content types and vendors, these experiences will differ widely.

- Data about the use case for the content (research, class assignment, entertainment, etc.) is largely up to the user sharing that information. This data can be useful, but it is only as strong as the data that is volunteered. Vendors will have different approaches, and many end users will choose not to submit feedback.

If publishers are transparent about these decisions, librarians can draw informed conclusions. Yet understanding the differences is time consuming and out of reach for libraries with limited staff. Those libraries and vendors who can take the time to pilot new approaches will help shape the metrics of the future. Initiatives in higher education, like IMS's Caliper Learning Analytics Framework (http://www.imsglobal.org/activity/caliper), are defining how to measure user engagement and learning impact. As universities are asked more and more to demonstrate learning outcomes, libraries will need to provide more meaningful analytics to demonstrate the value of electronic resources.

Next Steps
The referring data shown in the Alexander Street portal is especially revealing. Alexander Street reports the different sources of traffic to its resources and shares a deep dive in a special category called "Curated views." Curated views are a count-by-title of views received via user promotion: a Tweet, Facebook post, LibGuide embed, LMS embed, Wikipedia citation, and so on. Curated views:

- Indicate an investment on behalf of the person posting the link or embed, showing a deeper level of engagement.

- Count the users returning to the site and measure how successful these posts are at generating views.
- Demonstrate that the user community found value in the video and participated in its discovery.

Sharing this data opens avenues to learn more by comparing use from library referrals versus organic search. Do users coming from the library have a richer experience—for example, do they spend longer on each video, or engage more with each title? By connecting engagement metrics with referring data, libraries can see if efforts in discovery are leading to a deeper level of use.

There are additional opportunities to increase engagement by opening this data to the end user community directly. Vendors might share lists of highly rated videos or titles with the most overall engagement. Students can browse videos by "most-studied on campus" or "most frequently shown in classes." A heatmap on each video timeline could expose which sections of video are most popular or annotated for educational use.

However, multimedia is only one content type where these analytics can be reported. Because Alexander Street is now a ProQuest company, we have opportunities to look at a deeper engagement with books, journals, dissertations, and archives. For example, the Patron Analytics feature on Ebook Central—ProQuest's e-book platform—empowers libraries to add their own user surveys of one to five questions. When patrons complete these surveys, libraries can capture usage data on patrons' academic departments, geographic location, and academic role (e.g., student or faculty). Reports anonymize data and can be customized to collect and report on information that makes the biggest difference to the library.

Technology and insight in this area will continue to advance. Publishers know what can be reported, and librarians and faculty know what they should consider when assessing value. The most enduring possibilities will require true collaborations between publishers and the academic community.

Andrea Eastman-Mullins

ORCID ID: http://orcid.org/0000-0002-2978-7471

CONCLUSIONS

User engagement analytics should be seen as an addition to COUNTER usage reports, not as a replacement. For such analytics to be truly useful and respected, more work is needed on developing consistent standards for this type of reporting.

It can also be argued that more information and data may not always be a good thing, and libraries could run the risk of information overload hampering the very decision-making processes that they are trying to improve. Finding the "happy medium" between having enough data and being overloaded with data is something that can be achieved only through experience.

Ultimately, improving the understanding of how library users are engaging with resources is a worthy goal. When achieved, it will benefit everyone in the information community—libraries, publishers, and information consumers.

DATA-DRIVEN DECISION MAKING FOR ELECTRONIC RESOURCES

Priya Shenoy
Graduate Health Professions Librarian, Drake University,
priya.shenoy@drake.edu

Teri Koch
Head, Collection Development, Drake University,
teri.koch@drake.edu

Laura Krossner
Electronic Resources Manager, Drake University,
laura.krossner@drake.edu

ABSTRACT

The objective of the chapter is to determine common and best practices related to electronic resources analysis in academic libraries and how that information is used to inform retention and/or acquisition decisions. Using library literature and a survey of academic libraries, we identify characteristics and commonalities of effective electronic resource analysis processes.

Drake University has an effective process in place for electronic resource evaluation. We will compare our process to the survey results and determine common features and differences. We will put what we are doing in the context of the larger academic library profession.

INTRODUCTION

Like many other academic libraries facing years of budget stagnation or cuts and rising electronic resources pricing, Drake University's Cowles Library found itself in a crisis approximately five years ago. Cowles Library was barely able to fund inflation costs and was unable to add new resources requested by academic faculty unless a resource of equal or greater value was cancelled. Because this was an unsustainable model, Cowles Library created and

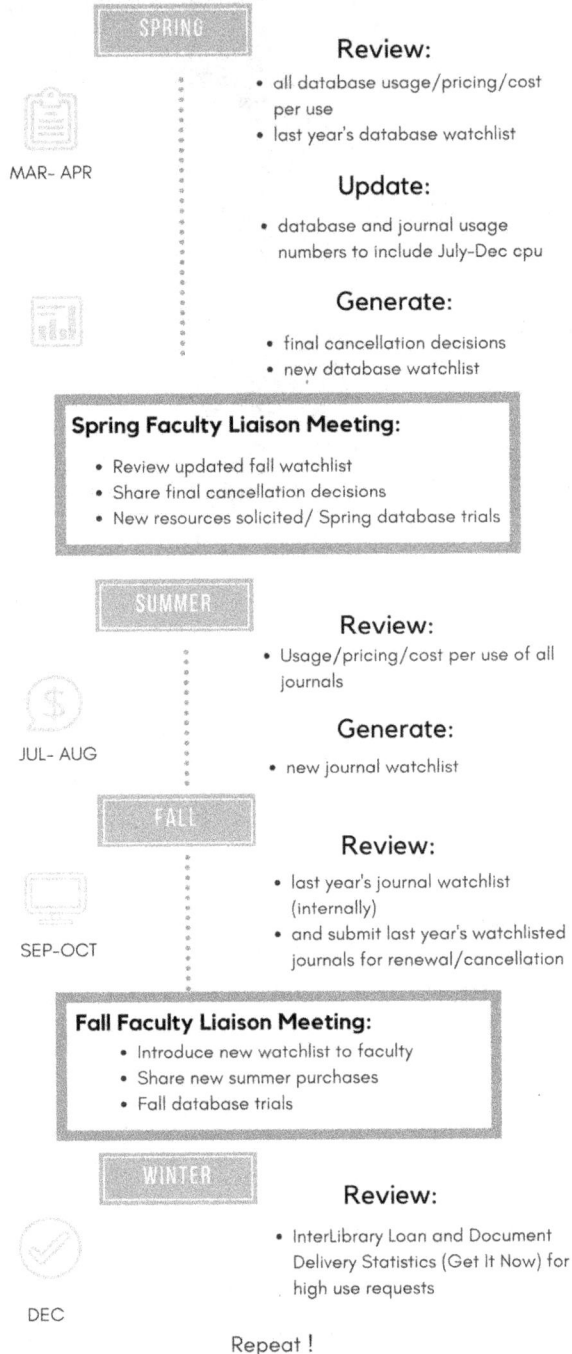

DRAKE UNIVERSITY ELECTRONIC RESOURCE EVALUATION

SPRING

MAR- APR

Review:
- all database usage/pricing/cost per use
- last year's database watchlist

Update:
- database and journal usage numbers to include July-Dec cpu

Generate:
- final cancellation decisions
- new database watchlist

Spring Faculty Liaison Meeting:
- Review updated fall watchlist
- Share final cancellation decisions
- New resources solicited/ Spring database trials

SUMMER

JUL- AUG

Review:
- Usage/pricing/cost per use of all journals

Generate:
- new journal watchlist

FALL

SEP-OCT

Review:
- last year's journal watchlist (internally)
- and submit last year's watchlisted journals for renewal/cancellation

Fall Faculty Liaison Meeting:
- Introduce new watchlist to faculty
- Share new summer purchases
- Fall database trials

WINTER

DEC

Review:
- InterLibrary Loan and Document Delivery Statistics (Get It Now) for high use requests

Repeat !

FIGURE 1. D(J)EG Cycle

undertook a yearly resource evaluation process to determine if the acquisitions budget was being spent on resources that were actually getting used. The new mantra became "the value of a resource is directly related to its usage."

In 2012, the Electronic Resources Selection Committee (ERSC) was formed to start reviewing usage data when resources came up for renewal. Since renewal dates were different for each subscription (aligning with the month it was started), the committee met monthly and looked at only a few resources at a time. This process was time consuming and made it difficult to compare resources across and within disciplines. Two factors changed the way this group worked: aligning the subscription dates for databases with the university's fiscal year (July 1–June 30), and better/more readily available COUNTER reports. As a result, the library has one major renewal period and the ability to compare usage across all electronic subscriptions against new pricing at the same time. COUNTER Release 4 provided ERSC with the ability to compare "apples to apples" when looking at usage across electronic subscriptions.

In 2014, the committee renamed itself Database (and Journals) Evaluation Group (D[J]EG) and created a cyclical review process for all electronic resource subscriptions (databases, journal packages, and single journal titles). The group follows a yearly calendar (described in Figure 1) to review all cost-per-use (CPU) data for resources to determine if that resource is going to be renewed, or renewed and watchlisted (see later for description of "Watchlists"). If a resource's CPU is above $25, that resource is watchlisted and shared with librarians and faculty. In particular, librarians and faculty are told that the watchlisted resource is under consideration for possible cancellation the following renewal year if usage does not improve. The reason $25 was decided upon as a threshold was because it matched the average amount spent per article on document delivery. For consistency sake, D(J)EG uses the $25 CPU threshold for both journal and database renewals.

ABOUT DRAKE UNIVERSITY

Drake University is a private, four-year university located in Des Moines, Iowa. The university's Carnegie Classification is Master's Large. The total student population in fall 2017 was 4,904 with 3,098 undergraduate and 1,806 graduate students at the master and doctoral levels. Student full-time equivalent (FTE) is at 4,191. About 120 undergraduate baccalaureate degrees are offered in a variety of disciplines. Sixty masters and four doctorate degrees are offered in professional studies (including law, pharmacy, occupational therapy, and education). In 2017, the Drake University Cowles Library budget was approximately $3.8 million with $1.5 million spent on acquisitions of materials in all formats.

LITERATURE REVIEW

Methods for evaluating electronic resources have evolved over the years since the advent of CD-ROM and floppy disk formats.

The reasons for undertaking review of electronic resources are well known in the library world: stagnant and/or shrinking budgets, inflation, and the ever-expanding number of resources available. Sutton (2013) mentioned that "the purpose of the analysis was to identify resources that might be candidates for future cancellations and to establish criteria for renewal and purchase decisions" (p. 245).

Kennedy et al. (2008) framed their analysis as a cost-savings measure and mentioned the rising costs of journals (especially in the sciences) and diminishing or flat budgets. Enoch and Harker (2015) had to undergo several rounds of cuts because of budget-related issues.

While collection development policies are relatively common for print materials, they are less common for electronic resources. Mangrum and Pozzebon (2012) discussed their review of 41 collection development policies and found that most policies focus on the selection rather than the life cycle of electronic resources. Gohn and Remy (2017) found that most libraries follow informal processes when selecting and reviewing electronic resources.

Foudy and McManus (2005) and Enoch and Harker (2015) both utilized decision grids to help with the decision-making process. Both can be adapted into continuous workflows. Gohn and Remy (2017) developed a holistic cyclical review process, looking at certain programs each year.

Most literature stresses the importance of involving teaching faculty in the review process, and sooner rather than later. Kennedy et al. (2008) communicated with faculty throughout their project and stressed the importance of a strong liaison process. Metz (1992) also stressed the importance of faculty input. One of the ways that Gohn and Remy (2017) involved teaching faculty in their project was by creating a watchlist of poorly performing titles (low usage and/or high CPU) and sharing that information with the faculty to raise awareness and solicit feedback. Enoch and Harker (2015) worked with teaching faculty extensively through multiple rounds of cuts.

Several different criteria and factors were considered throughout these various electronic resource evaluation projects. Sutton (2013) employed two levels of analysis. The first level consisted of various usage data, including searches, sessions, full-text downloads, and link-outs, all analyzed over multiple years. When necessary, a second level of analysis was employed, consisting of overlap, citations, journal usage, and impact factor data.

Kennedy et al. (2008) considered usage statistics, CPU, scope, and impact factor of journals. They also considered the availability of document delivery options for expensive but low-use titles. CPU was the primary decision factor.

Foudy and McManus (2005) developed a criteria-based decision grid. Before deploying the grid, they created a "core" list of titles that were protected from cancellation. This list accounted for 75% of expenditures. The decision grid takes objective and subjective measures and forces a ranking structure that allows for more objective decision making. The rankings were provided by subject teams based upon these criteria: access, cost-effectiveness, breadth/audience, and uniqueness.

Enoch and Harker (2015) discussed three rounds of cuts at University of North Texas. In the first round, they moved approval plans to "slip only" and converted their print collection to electronic where possible. In the second round, they considered duplication between print and electronic, duplication across resources, and looked closely at resources whose access was limited to certain categories of users. They also looked at usage and anything with a high CPU (which they deemed to be $71). This process created a "Master Cut" list that could be shared with subject liaisons and teaching faculty. They found that the use of both objective and subjective data was especially helpful in creating faculty "buy-in." In the third round, they looked at subscriptions with costs of $1,000 or greater and also looked more closely at "Big Deals." They considered alternative scenarios for each package, including a combination of subscribing to low CPU titles and offering alternative access to mid-CPU titles, such as document delivery options.

Gohn and Remy (2017) developed a cyclical review period for review of their resources but only looked at certain programs/subject areas each year. One of their approaches included doing an environmental scan of their peer institutions. They presented scenarios that discussed cancelling underutilized resources and replacing them with resources thought to be more relevant to the curriculum.

Gohn and Remy reported "next steps" as attempting to generate more awareness of resources through subject guides, considering the possibility of joint funding with departments, and including funding requests in new degree and grant proposals. They are also considering tying usage to institutional measures such as student credit hours, faculty FTE, and number of majors within a department (to make better arguments for increased funding or cancellation of resources).

To summarize, there are obviously many methods utilized in conducting electronic resource evaluation projects. These methods run the gamut from informal, one-time projects to more formalized and cyclical processes. Most utilize both objective and subjective data to arrive at decisions. The most common objective data considered is resource usage (often averaged over three to five years), and CPU. Other objective data considered includes number of sessions, number of searches, full-text downloads, record views, link-outs, overlap with other resources, citations, impact factor, scope of resource, embargoes, inflation, and availability via document delivery. The most common subjective data considered when reviewing e-resources is ranking by subject librarians and/or teaching faculty, accreditation standards, access issues (technical reliability, ease of setting up link resolver, ease of use for patrons), and an environmental scan of peer institutions.

Most institutions stress the importance of the involvement of both subject librarians and teaching faculty in the evaluation process. Many discuss sharing spreadsheets for ranking purposes, LibGuides, e-mails, and setting up watchlists of underutilized titles.

OVERVIEW OF COWLES LIBRARY'S D(J)EG PROCESS

Cowles Library's current database and journal evaluation process has evolved to its current formal and cyclical state, with a strong emphasis on participation by both librarians and subject faculty.

One of the first major tasks the group undertook was aligning the majority of database renewals with the fiscal year. This saved D(J)EG time and allowed the group to consider data from multiple disciplines for a broader perspective. Additionally, it greatly simplified budget expenditure tracking, since the entire invoice amount is assigned to one fiscal year. Since journal renewals run on a calendar year, they are reviewed separately from databases.

Cowles Library has an active reciprocal library liaison program, which serves as a critical communication channel between the library and other campus faculty. A librarian liaison is assigned to each college at Drake (in the case of the College of Arts & Sciences, each department). Likewise, each college (or department) assigns one of its faculty members to the liaison program.

D(J)EG PROCESS–PHASES

Spring (April/May)

- D(J)EG reviews the watchlist (see "Watchlists" later in the chapter) from the prior fall after the electronic resources librarian updates it with the most recent usage data. This is the final chance for resources to be saved by improved usage data. Final renewal/cancelation decisions are made.

- Final cancelation decisions are announced at the spring liaison meeting via the updated watchlist.

- New unmet resource needs are solicited at the spring liaison meeting for March trial database period.

- As invoices come in for the fiscal year period beginning July 1, D(J) EG begins reviewing pricing, usage, and CPU for each and creates a new watchlist to be shared at the fall liaison meeting.

Summer (July/August)

- Journal renewals arrive. D(J)EG reviews pricing, usage, and CPU for each title.

- New journal watchlist is created for poor CPU titles (the watchlist is "private" until the fall liaison meeting when those with the direct URL will be able to view the page).

Fall (September/October)

- Journal/database watchlist is shared at the fall liaison meeting.

- Subject faculty liaisons are expected to share this information with their departmental colleagues: if usage doesn't improve, the resource(s) on the watchlist will be cancelled in the spring.

- D(J)EG reviews the updated journal usage and CPU for journals on the watchlist one last time to see if there has been any improvement. If not, the title is cancelled.

Winter (December/January)

- D(J)EG reviews interlibrary loan and document delivery statistics and costs to determine if it would be more economical to start a journal subscription rather than acquiring by the article. Note: starting a new subscription has rarely happened.

As Needed: Electronic journals and subscription databases make up the majority of the resources that are reviewed in the D(J)EG process. However, there are a few other categories that are also reviewed:

- Print subscriptions (every three years)
- Print standing orders (as needed)
- One-time database purchases (as needed)

Watchlists

A watchlist is the primary vehicle for outward communication for D(J)EG. This information is shared via the library liaison program in the fall and in the spring. As mentioned earlier, a watchlist is created when a journal or database experiences a CPU >$25. A sample watchlist can be viewed at http://researchguides.drake.edu/charleston2017.

There are multiple criteria listed on the watchlist for each resource, including renewal cost total, usage for each of the prior three years (including year-to-date), CPU for each of the prior three years, and, for databases, a chart that shows a trendline for ideal CPU versus actual CPU. The watchlist is shared within the library's Springshare LibGuides and is set to private so only those with a direct URL can view the information.

Additional Watchlist Factors

In addition to the criteria mentioned earlier, there are often additional factors taken into consideration by D(J)EG when making a determination whether or not to watchlist a resource:

- Trend lines over multiple years (for both usage and CPU)
- Does the resource align with university strategic priorities, for example, diversity and inclusion initiative, community engagement (e.g., ProQuest Black Studies Center)?
- Are there specific accreditation requirements that require retaining the resource(s) even if usage/CPU is poor (e.g., ACS journals)?

- Number of resources for and size of the department. Drake has several relatively small departments with expensive resources, especially in the mathematics and physics area. Many of the journals in these areas have been cancelled due to high CPU. D(J)EG is reluctant to eliminate the one major database (e.g., MathSciNet, IOPScience journals) in each discipline based on high CPU alone.
- Is the disciplinary area new and/or growing at Drake? Often resources are given additional time to meet the desired CPU threshold if the area is one that has been recently added to the Drake curriculum.

Obtaining New Resources

Using the process described earlier, along with reallocated book acquisitions funds, Cowles Library was able to identify over $175,000 between fiscal years 2015 and 2017 to help offset inflation and to fund new electronic learning resources. Subject faculty were actively involved in identifying desired new resources via the liaison process. In fact, the possibility of adding new and needed resources motivated subject faculty involvement in the watchlist process.

The main factors considered in obtaining a new electronic resource are listed on the library's web page. They include:

- Budget availability
- Curriculum support (what need does this resource fill that is not currently being met?)
- One-time purchase versus ongoing subscription (preference given to one-time purchase)
- Requesting a trial in either the fall (October) or spring (March)
- Review of feedback received during the trial period
- Additional criteria considered are listed here: https://library.drake. edu/wp-content/blogs.dir/1/files/2015/07/ER-Evaluation-Factors-Drake-version-final-10-19-17.xlsx

Challenges

While overall the D(J)EG committee is satisfied with the process established for electronic resource evaluation, there are some ongoing challenges. First, the process has identified the "low-hanging fruit" in terms of poor-performing resources. At this point, the remaining resources have either relatively favorable CPU or are in one of the "other" categories mentioned earlier. At this point, Cowles Library is barely able to identify enough resources to cancel to cover inflation costs. While it is satisfying that the majority of the remaining resources are doing well, this process is not sustainable going forward.

An additional challenge experienced by D(J)EG is marketing underutilized resources. One of the reasons the group watchlists a resource is to increase faculty awareness, and therefore, hopefully, increase usage. Direct e-mails are also sent to stakeholder subject faculty. In terms of campus-wide marketing, D(J)EG has tried multiple methods (e.g., blog posts on the library webpage, blog posts on a university campus-wide newsletter, and slides on the main library webpage). So far, none of these methods have proven to be hugely successful. D(J)EG hopes to find other ways to work more directly with the subject faculty via the library liaison process to increase awareness of and utilization of these resources.

Survey Methods

In order to gain further insight into practices that are currently being employed to inform retention and/or acquisition decisions, we developed a survey on common practices regarding electronic resource evaluation in academic libraries. After receiving Institutional Review Board (IRB) approval, we distributed the survey to the following listservs: ERIL, Serials -T, TRAC, as well as individuals who registered to attend the presentation on D(J)EG's process given at the 2017 Charleston Conference. The individuals in these groups were determined to be the most pertinent to answer these questions because of their involvement with electronic resource analysis. The survey took approximately 10 minutes to complete and consisted of 20 questions. The questions were a mixture of multiple-choice, multiple-answer, matrix table, and open-ended questions (see survey questions in the Appendix). The survey instrument was shared with three librarian colleagues to test for content and context validity.

Survey Results

Demographics

The survey received 105 responses during the three-week time frame it was active. The first three questions asked for academic institutional demographic information. Of the responses, 50% were from public institutions, and 50% were from private. Academic full-time equivalents (FTEs) varied greatly by institution. The biggest response group came from 0 to 2,500 FTE, with 33% of respondents. The other categories received fairly equal responses (14–18% by category). Carnegie Classification of Institutions yielded generally even results, with 41% at the doctoral level, 35% at master's, and 24% at baccalaureate. Demographics were fairly evenly distributed across categories, which allows for good representation of data. The summary begged the following question: what does the data look like parsed by each demographic category of private versus public institution; FTE size; and Carnegie Classification? Therefore, this information is also addressed in the sections that follow. (Note: Not all numbers add up to 100% due to nonresponse rate.)

Budget Trends

Across three years of reported data, 22% of academic libraries reported a budget increase. During the same time period, 76% of academic libraries indicated either a budget decrease or budget stagnation. We categorize budget decreases and stagnation as equivalent since stagnation does not take into account standard yearly inflation/price increases, resulting in a negative budget balance if methods aren't employed to counteract this. The respondents in the categories of public versus private, Carnegie Classification, and FTE size all showed a trend toward budget stagnation throughout each of the past three fiscal years, and a trend toward budget decrease regardless of public versus private, baccalaureate and master's institutions, and all FTE sizes except 25,001+. Doctoral Carnegie Classification and 25,001+ FTE were the only groups who reported a trend toward budget increases. Generally, the schools with smaller FTEs indicated trends toward budget stagnation and budget decreases. The largest percentage of respondents, across all FTE categories, responded that their budget was stagnant for each of the past three fiscal years, with responses varying from 41% to 68%. The category "Our budget was stagnant" was also the most statistically prevalent throughout each Carnegie Classification. The "Our budget was stagnant" category for Baccalaureate institutions declined over three years, while the "Our budget decreased" category rose from 18% in FY16 to 27% in FY17 to 45% in FY18.

Renewal/Cancellation Criteria

When considering common methods and criteria used to inform the electronic resource subscription renewal/selection/cancellation process, there

FY18

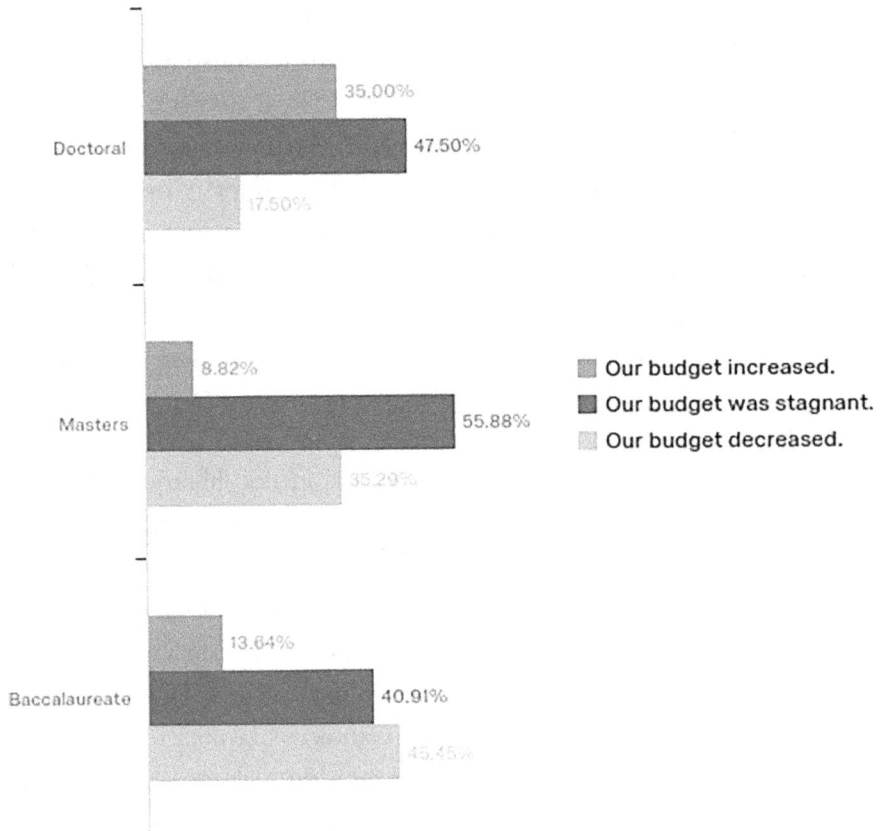

FIGURE 2A. Budget by Carnegie Classification FY16–FY18

were some clear patterns. A majority (88%) of respondents stated that librarian review of electronic subscription costs and CPU are often useful or mostly useful. A majority (61%) indicated that faculty review of subscriptions was rarely or never used. Most baccalaureate programs (83%) said that considering whether a disciplinary area is growing or declining is a criterion that is often or most often used.

One limitation of the survey instrument was that review of cost and CPU were listed together as one item in one of the questions instead of being listed as two separate choices. Therefore, it is difficult to determine if librarians use CPU or cost alone as a main factor for their decision-making process. This issue is further explored in an open-ended question later in the survey.

FY17

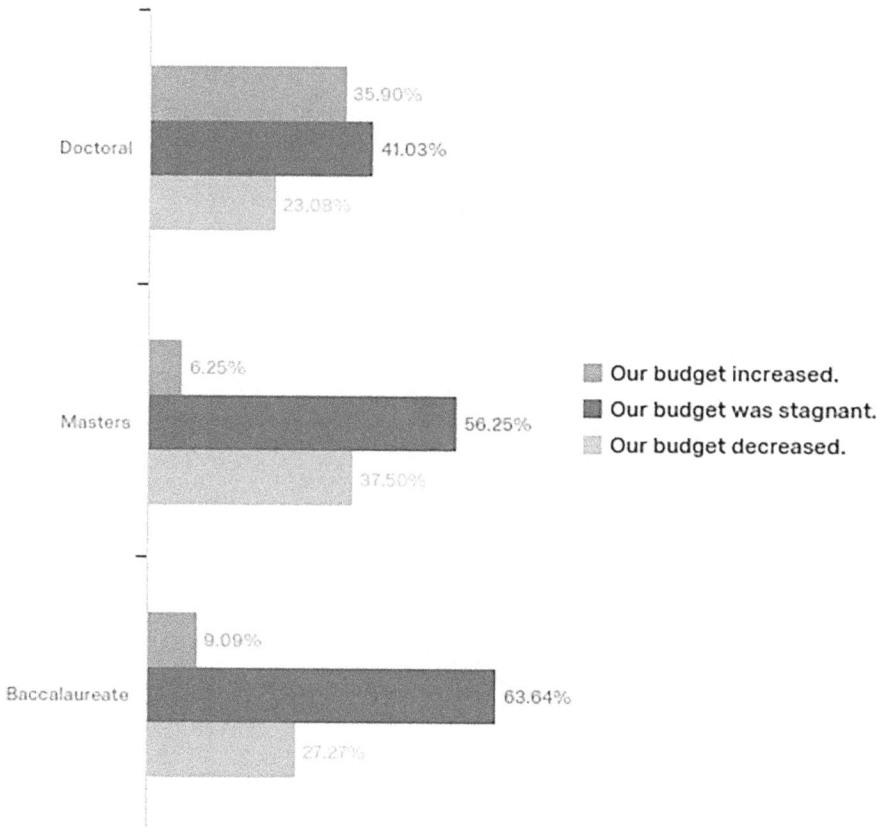

FIGURE 2B. Continued

The open-ended written responses regarding other methods or criteria indicated that there are institutions that pay close attention to faculty research and publication patterns. The area that received the most mentions in written statements (especially for public, doctoral, and larger FTE institutions) was related to citation analysis of faculty and student research at the respondent's institution. Other areas mentioned were faculty determination of their most relevant journals, journal impact factor, cost to obtain via interlibrary loan and/or document delivery, whether it is used in class assignments, frequency of interlibrary loan requests, consistent price/inflation increases, and overall use of item (not CPU). One response noted that their institution considers

FY16

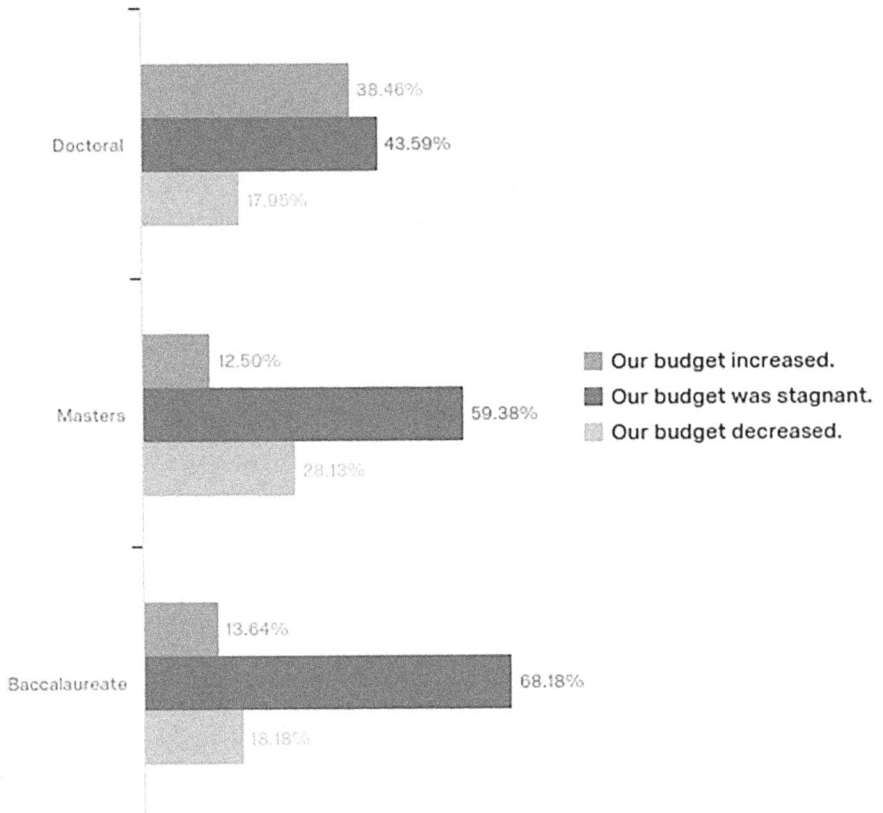

FIGURE 2C. Continued

"vendor commitment to values of diversity, inclusion, and social justice," which is a method the authors of this chapter had not previously considered.

The survey asked respondents to describe their electronic renewal/selection/cancellation process as an open-ended question. The two themes that arose specifically in terms of selecting new resources were canceling a resource of similar value in order to fund a new resource and participating in a trial of a resource before purchasing/subscribing to it.

In contrast to the selection process, there were multiple factors mentioned when specifically considering renewing or cancelling a resource. Some institutions only consider renewal factors as needed (e.g., when budget cuts arise), but many libraries review on some sort of cycle (every X years, every year, etc.) The most commonly considered factors for renewal are usage, CPU,

TABLE 1. Renewal/cancellation criteria

Field	1 = not used		2 = rarely useful		3 = occasionally useful		4 = often useful		5 = most useful	
Accreditation requirements	8.08%	8	13.13%	13	30.30%	30	31.31%	31	17.17%	17
Add a resource and cancel a resource of equal cost	6.12%	6	14.29%	14	48.98%	48	22.45%	22	8.16%	8
Compatibility and integration with your discovery service	14.14%	14	16.16%	16	32.32%	32	27.27%	27	10.10%	10
Faculty review of subscriptions in their subject area with a dollar target to cut	27.27%	27	33.33%	33	21.21%	21	14.14%	14	4.04%	4
Is discipline area associated with the resource growing or declining at your institution?	5.05%	5	8.08%	8	33.33%	33	31.31%	31	22.22%	22
Librarian review of electronic subscription costs as well as cost per use numbers to make a renewal decision	1.01%	1	2.02%	2	9.09%	9	41.41%	41	46.46%	46
Librarian review of subscriptions with a dollar target to cut	7.07%	7	18.18%	18	32.32%	32	33.33%	33	9.09%	9
Usability or functionailty of resource	2.02%	2	7.07%	7	40.40%	40	34.34%	34	16.16%	16

cost, price increase, overlap with other active library subscriptions (either specific titles or general content), and alignment with curriculum/specific classes
taught at institution. Most institutions report using multiple factors simultaneously. A few schools use a specific threshold to determine if the resource
is poorly utilized. Two schools mentioned $35, one school $100, and two
others mentioned that they have a threshold but either didn't report a dollar
amount or noted that it changes by subject/discipline.

One previously discussed limitation of the survey instrument is potential
combination of cost and CPU or usage and CPU. It is unclear if respondents
were using the terms of usage and CPU interchangeably in their responses.
Similarly, when responses included both cost and usage, it is possible that
institutions used both to calculate CPU (either informally or formally) but
did not report this as part of their answer.

Communication

Many schools mentioned communication, both between librarians and
between the library and faculty. Almost all reported reciprocal communication where, after the information was shared, librarians and/or faculty could
weigh in with their opinions and concerns. One respondent said, "We have
found making the process as democratic as possible with as many faculty as
possible engaged in the decisions works best, though it can be unwieldy and
time consuming." Other respondents mentioned times they tried to share
cancellation information but were inundated with complaints from faculty.
One response to another question stated, "Faculty are almost never informed
of cancellations, formally or informally," with the same respondent reporting
(for a different question) that "faculty are rarely consulted on cancellations
of electronic information services. Many are still caught up in the era of core
resources, not whether the resources are actually used."

Most respondents (62%) to an open-ended question reported that they
do not have an articulated process for evaluating electronic resources at their
institution. Private institutions are more likely to have an articulated process
than public (41% vs. 20%). A number of respondents wrote that they plan to
create a process document in the future.

One survey question specifically asked about the extent of the involvement of subject faculty (referred to in survey as "Non-Librarian Teaching

Faculty") and librarians in the electronic subscription renewal decision-making process. The results of this question show a strong emphasis on communication in its various forms, formal as well as informal, throughout the process. We hoped to determine if there was a difference in responses related to formal liaison programs versus more informal processes. The results show that both are common and that information flows in multiple directions.

Overall, more than 86% of respondents indicated that librarian communication with subject faculty via a formal liaison process is moderately or very important (54% said it's very important). A majority (88%) of respondents indicated it's moderately or very important that individual subject faculty (not faculty liaisons) communicate with librarians informally.

These results imply that communication is important both as a part of a formal liaison process and outside of that process. Further, 81% of responses show that subject faculty liaison communication with their faculty colleagues is either moderately or very important.

The major differences in responses by demographics were seen in the category "Individual subject faculty communicate with librarians informally." For public institutions, 47% indicated this was "very important." Only 5% said it was "not important." For private institutions, only 26% indicated this was "very important," and 21% said it was "not important." It is interesting to see that informal communication initiated by subject faculty is much more relevant in public institutions than private institutions. The other area that showed some differentiation was related to the category "Subject faculty liaison communicates with their faculty." In public institutions, 61% of respondents indicated this was "very important," and only 14% said it was "not important." For private institutions, on the other hand, only 36% of respondents indicated it was "very important," and 27% indicated it was "not important." It appears that public institutions rely more on subject faculty communicating with their peers to disseminate information, and more emphasis is placed on other methods in private institutions (including the formal liaison process).

Analysis by FTE shows that "librarian communicates with subject faculty via formal liaison process" was very important across almost all FTEs. Note the drop in perceived importance from the 10,001–25,000 category to the 25,001+ category. However, 50% of the respondents in that largest FTE

Individual subject faculty communicate with librarians informally

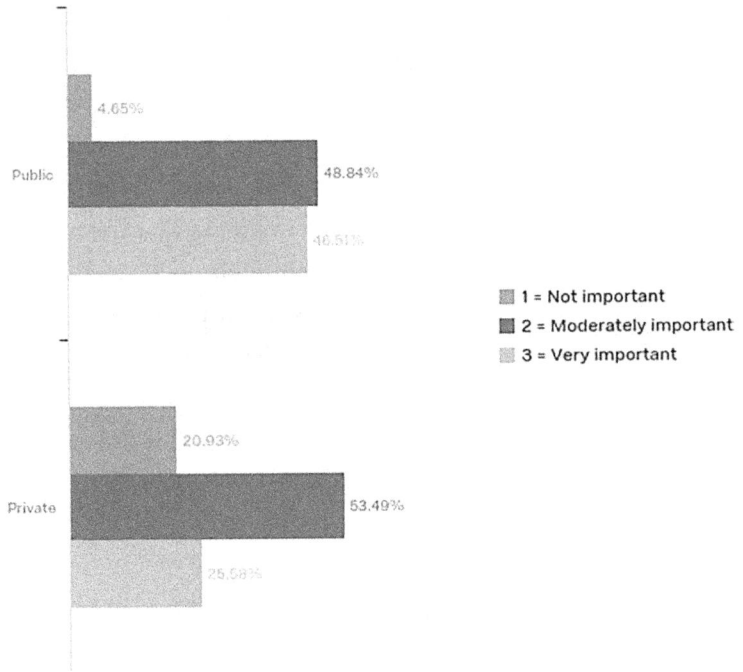

Public
- 4.65%
- 48.84%
- 46.51%

1 = Not important
2 = Moderately important
3 = Very important

Private
- 20.93%
- 53.49%
- 25.58%

Subject faculty liaison communicates with their faculty

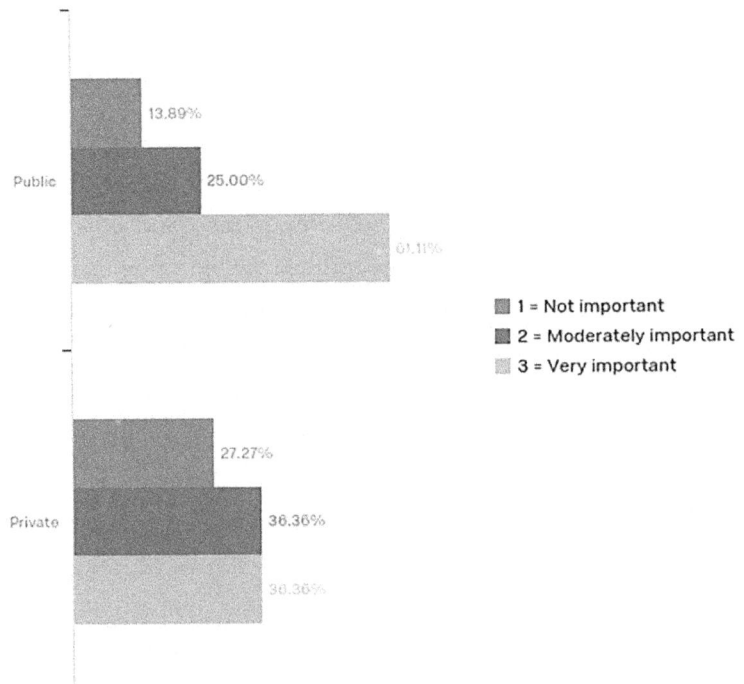

Public
- 13.89%
- 25.00%
- 61.11%

1 = Not important
2 = Moderately important
3 = Very important

Private
- 27.27%
- 36.36%
- 36.36%

FIGURE 3. Subject faculty communication—public/private

Librarian communicates with subject faculty via formal liaison process

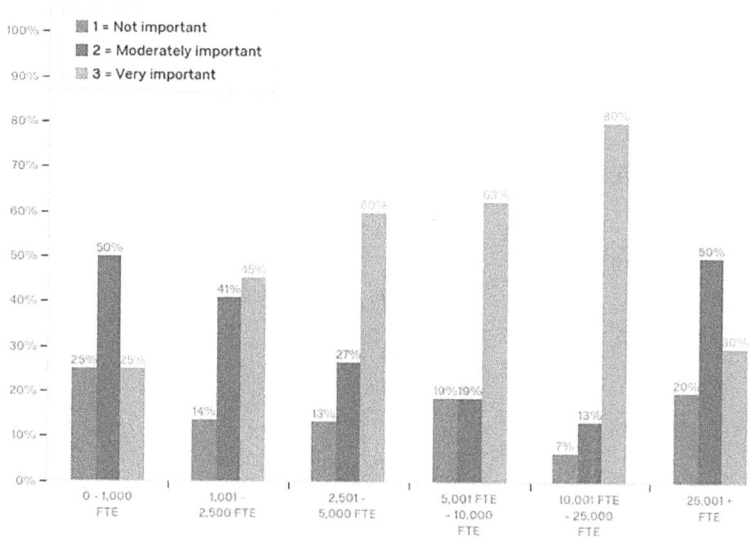

FIGURE 4. Librarian communication—FTE

category did rate it "moderately important." This begs the question, are formal liaison programs not used as frequently in larger institutions?

Subject Faculty Involvement

The authors discovered another limitation of the survey instrument when asking an open-ended question about other methods used involving subject faculty in the electronic subscription renewal decision-making process. The authors grouped renewal, selection, and cancellation processes into the same category, primarily because at their institution, these processes are essentially part of the same workflow, as they directly affect each other. Most respondents indicated that they do not involve subject faculty in the renewal process, but rather only in the cancellation process, and some only in specific instances. Some respondents indicated they reach out to faculty only if the resource they are considering cancelling has moderate-to-high usage, or if the item has traditionally been considered a "core" resource.

When asked specifically about methods used to communicate with subject faculty, e-mail/phone is the primary method of communication, followed by informal meetings and dissemination of resource evaluation lists. It is clear from responses that multiple methods are often employed simultaneously. As

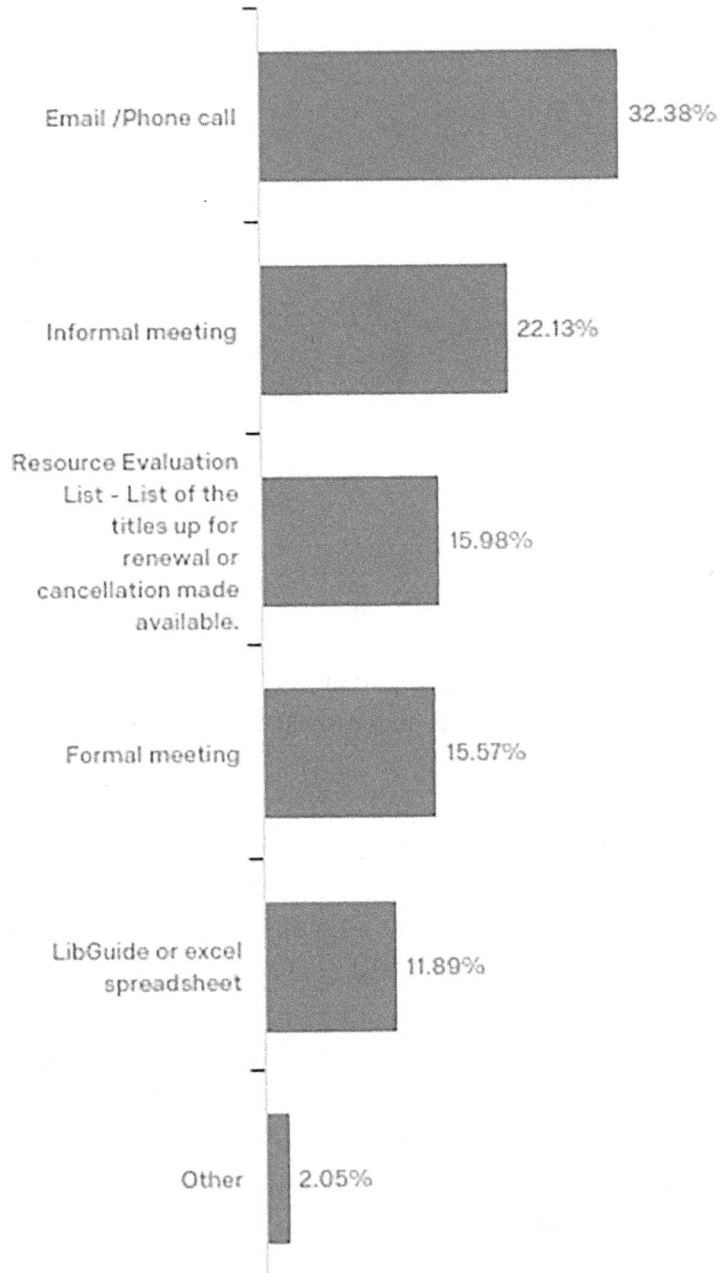

FIGURE 5. Methods of communication

was mentioned in the "Communication" section earlier, renewal, cancellation, and resource evaluation all have differing levels of faculty contact. Common methods mentioned in the open-ended comments included using the library website and newsletters. The smallest FTE group (0–2,500) places the highest importance on multiple forms of communication (LibGuide or Excel [39%]; formal meetings [38%]; and resource evaluation lists [42%] were the highest). Other FTEs average 10–22% for each category. Public institutions place more importance on meetings (both formal and informal) than private institutions (62% vs. 38%, respectively).

Adding New Resources

Requests from faculty were considered the most important method for identifying new electronic resource subscriptions (73%). This was followed by requests from librarians (40%), subject review/gap analysis (26%), and lastly by a demonstration from a company representative (3%). Other methods were listed via an open-ended response option. A few individuals also listed

Importance of Requests from Faculty

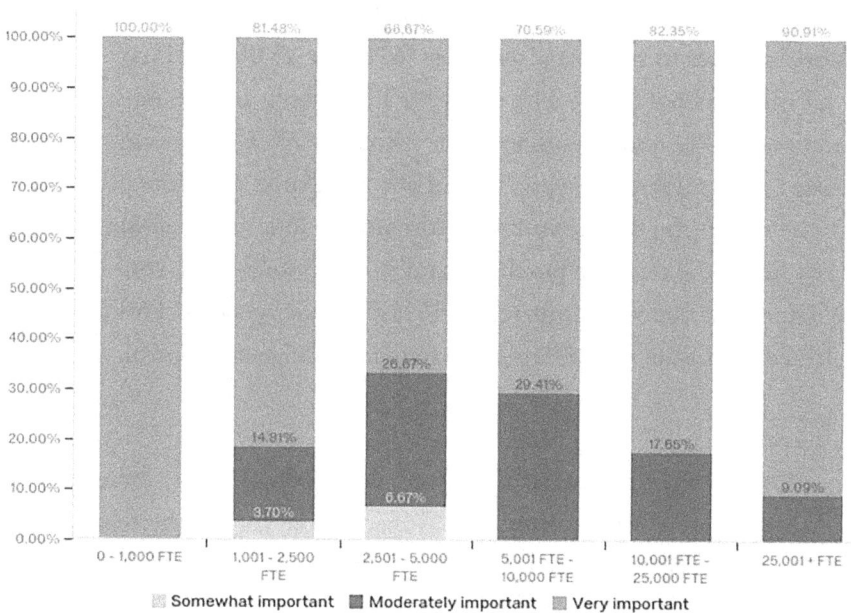

FIGURE 6. Importance of requests from faculty

requests from students as moderately to somewhat important. Other items that were mentioned were high interlibrary loan requests for a resource, benchmarking with other institutions (particularly for new programs), and learning about resources through library literature. A few also mentioned that they were not adding resources due to budgetary constraints. Doctoral and public institutions were the only type to mention the importance of student requests (except for one private baccalaureate institution that accepts student requests for e-book titles). In general, the larger the FTE, the more importance institutions place on resource requests from faculty. (See Figure 6.)

The survey asked about common methods of funding new electronic resources subscriptions or large one-time purchases. All the methods listed in the survey instrument are utilized to some degree by libraries. The most useful method is cancelling poor CPU resources (93% classified this as moderately or very important). The second most useful method is cancelling a resource of similar value (86%), followed closely by internally reallocating budgets (e.g., spending less money on books) (84%). The least useful methods were relying on budget increases or grants/external funding, as it is difficult for libraries to secure these. In an open-ended comment, a few libraries mentioned that end-of-year monies are used for making large, one-time purchases.

Broken out by demographic categories, the largest FTE schools can rely on budget increases to fund new resources (67% for 25,001+ FTEs vs. 0–40% for all other school sizes). The smaller FTE schools are the most likely to cancel poor CPU resources than larger schools (70% FTEs less than 10,000 reported this method as very important, compared to 56% of 10,001+ FTEs). Private schools place more importance on internally reallocating budgets to fund new resource purchases and subscriptions (58% consider this a very important method compared to 36% of public schools). This is perhaps explained by private schools often having more budgetary control.

Observations

When comparing the process employed by Cowles Library for electronic resource evaluation with processes identified in the survey, there were some general notable differences.

First, the process D(J)EG employs is both cyclical and formal. It is cyclical in that there are particular events that will occur at a specific time and place in the cycle (as outlined earlier), and it is formal in that the process has been established and communicated through the library liaison program for the past four years. Many respondents (though not all) noted that their process is not yet cyclical or formal, though many responses indicated that this is the direction they are headed.

There are many data points being considered by institutions in the electronic resource evaluation process. Certainly, usage and CPU are two of the most common. There are also a variety of objective and subjective factors. Undoubtedly, this makes coming up with a defined and formal process more difficult.

The amount and level of involvement of subject faculty in the process varied greatly by institution. Most schools did indicate involvement of subject faculty at some point in the process, but overall this varied. Several responses indicated that library liaison programs are no longer employed (this trended toward larger institutions). One response from a public institution stressed the importance of the subject faculty liaison reaching out to their own faculty, but that a lot of the time this either doesn't happen or isn't communicated back to the library.

CONCLUSION

At many institutions, electronic resource subscriptions make up a large percentage of the acquisitions budget. At Drake University, they represent over 90% of the acquisitions budget. Based on the survey results, most schools use a variety of methods for evaluating electronic resource subscriptions. It is the authors' conclusion that as budgets continue to stagnate or decline it is more important than ever to articulate a data-driven decision process for electronic resource renewals that is both cyclical and formal with as much involvement and communication with subject faculty as possible or feasible. Furthermore, there will soon be new COUNTER R5 reports available that show promise for collecting new data points for analysis.

While not a panacea (as mentioned, once the low-hanging fruit is plucked, it can be hard to identify resources to cut), the process is vital to maintaining access to the resources most used and needed by students and faculty in this era of stagnant and declining budgets.

ACKNOWLEDGMENT

Special thanks to Mary Pat Wohlford and Christine Marchand at Drake University for their assistance with our qualtrics survey!

BIBLIOGRAPHY

Enoch, Todd, and Karen R. Harker. 2015. "Planning for the Budget-ocalypse: The Evolution of a Serials/ER Cancellation Methodology." *Serials Librarian* 68, no. 1–4: 282–289. https://doi.org/10.1080/0361526X.2015.1025657

Foudy, Gerry and Alesia McManus. 2005. "Using a Decision Grid Process to Build Consensus in Electronic Resources Cancellation Decisions." *Journal Of Academic Librarianship* 31, no. 6: 533–538. https://doi.org/10.1016/j.acalib.2005.08.005

Gohn, Katie, and Charlie Remy. 2017. "Proactive and Prudent: A Report of a Holistic Cyclical Electronic Resources Review Pilot at the University of Tennessee at Chattanooga." *Serials Librarian* 73, no. 1: 44–52. https://doi.org/10.1080/0361526X.2017.1309335

Kennedy, Kathryn, Tara Tobin Cataldo, Valrie Davis, Sara Russell Gonzalez, and Carrie Newsom. 2008. "Evaluating Continuing Resources: Perspectives and Methods from Science Librarians." *Serials Librarian* 55, no. 3: 428–443. https://doi.org/10.1080/03615260802059064

Mangrum, Suzanne, and Mary Ellen Pozzebon. 2012. "Use of Collection Development Policies in Electronic Resource Management." *Collection Building* 31, no. 3: 108–114. https://doi.org/10.1108/01604951211243506

Metz, Paul. 1992. "Thirteen Steps to Avoiding Bad Luck in a Serials." *Journal of Academic Librarianship* 18, no. 2: 76. *Academic Search Premier*, EBSCO*host* (accessed July 25, 2018).

Shenoy, Priya, Laura Krossner, and Teri Koch. 2017. "Money Doesn't Grow on Trees": Using a Data-Driven Review Process to Add New Resources with No Budget Increases. *Charleston Conference Proceedings*. In press.

Sutton, Sarah. 2013. "A Model for Electronic Resources Value Assessment." *Serials Librarian* 64, no. 1–4: 245–253. https://doi.org/10.1080/0361526X.2013.760417

Academic Library Electronic Resources
Evaluation Survey

What type of institution are you?

- Public (1)
- Private (2)

What is your institution's Full-Time Equivalent (FTE) enrollment?

- 0–1,000 FTE (1)
- 1,001–2,500 FTE (2)
- 2,501–5,000 FTE (3)
- 5,001 FTE – 10,000 FTE (4)
- 10,001 FTE – 25,000 FTE (5)
- 25,001 + FTE (6)

Which of these best describes your "Carnegie Classification of Institutions" for higher education? (http://carnegieclassifications.iu.edu/classification_descriptions/basic.php)

- Doctoral (1)
- Masters (2)
- Baccalaureate (3)

Please answer the following related to your acquisitions budget over the past three years.

	Our budget increased. (1)	Our budget was stagnant. (2)	Our budget decreased. (3)
FY 2018 (1)	○	○	○
FY 2017 (2)	○	○	○
FY 2016 (3)	○	○	○

Listed below are some common methods and criteria used to help inform the electronic resource subscription renewal/selection/cancellation process. Please rank each method or criterion in terms of its usefulness to you in making these renewal decisions. (1 being not used and 5 being the most useful)

	1 = Not Used (1)	2 = Rarely Useful (2)	3 = Occasionally Useful (3)	4 = Often Useful (4)	5 = Most Useful (5)
Add a resource and cancel a resource of equal cost. (1)	○	○	○	○	○
Librarian review of subscriptions with a dollar target to cut. (2)	○	○	○	○	○
Faculty review of subscriptions in their subject area with a dollar target to cut. (3)	○	○	○	○	○
Librarian review of electronic subscription costs as well as cost per use numbers to make a renewal decision. (4)	○	○	○	○	○
Accreditation requirements. (5)	○	○	○	○	○
Usability or functionailty of resource. (6)	○	○	○	○	○
Compatibility and integration with your discovery service. (7)	○	○	○	○	○
Is discipline area associated with the resource growing or declining at your institution? (8)	○	○	○	○	○

If you use a method or criterion that was not listed in the question above, please state the method and rate its usefulness using the scale above.

_____

_____

_____

_____

_____

Please describe your electronic resource evaluation processes and indicate those that are most effective.

_____

_____

_____

_____

_____

Do you have articulated processes that direct or describe how you approach electronic resource evaluation at your institution? If so, please provide a link or write a description.

_____

_____

_____

_____

_____

Many academic libraries involve subject faculty in the electronic subscription renewal decision-making process. Please indicate the importance of the methods below in your process.

	1 = Not important (1)	2 = Moderately important (2)	3 = Very important (3)	Not applicable (4)
Librarians communicate with subject faculty via formal liaison process. (1)	○	○	○	○
Librarians communicate with subject faculty informally. (2)	○	○	○	○
A designated subject faculty liaison communicates with librarians via formal liaison process. (3)	○	○	○	○

(Continued)

(Continued)

	1 = Not important (1)	2 = Moderately important (2)	3 = Very important (3)	Not applicable (4)
Individual subject faculty communicate with librarians informally. (4)	○	○	○	○
Subject faculty liaison communicates with their faculty. (5)	○	○	○	○

If you do not use any of the methods listed above, please describe the method you use and indicate its importance.

_____
_____
_____
_____
_____

Relating to the previous question, which of the following methods do you use to communicate with subject faculty (select all that apply)?

- Resource Evaluation List – List of the titles up for renewal or cancellation made available. (1)
- Email /Phone call (2)
- Formal meeting (3)
- Informal meeting (4)
- LibGuide or excel spreadsheet (5)
- Other (6)
- Not applicable (7)

Display This Question:
If Relating to the previous question, which of the following methods do you use to communicate with. . . = Other
If you selected other, please describe below.

_____
_____
_____
_____
_____

Below are common methods for identifying options for new electronic resource subscriptions. Please indicate the importance of the methods below in your process.

	Somewhat important (1)	Moderately important (2)	Very important (3)	Not applicable (4)
Requests from Faculty (1)	○	○	○	○
Requests from Librarian (2)	○	○	○	○
Subject Review/Gap analysis (3)	○	○	○	○
Demonstration from representative (4)	○	○	○	○

If other methods are used, please describe the method and indicate its importance.

_____

_____

_____

_____

_____

What percent of the time do you require a trial before purchasing or subscribing to a new electronic resource?

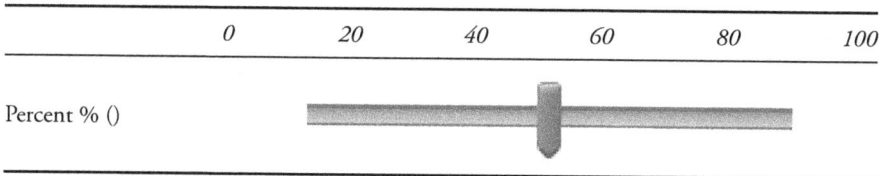

	0	20	40	60	80	100
Percent % ()						

Below are common methods of funding new electronic resource subscriptions (or large one-time purchases). Please indicate the importance of the methods below in your process.

	Somewhat important (1)	Moderately important (2)	Very important (3)	Not Applicable (4)
Cancel a resource of similar value (1)	○	○	○	○
Internally reallocate budget lines (eg: purchase fewer print books) (2)	○	○	○	○

(Continued)

(Continued)

	Somewhat important (1)	Moderately important (2)	Very important (3)	Not Applicable (4)
Rely on budget increase (3)	○	○	○	○
Cancel poor cost per use resources (4)	○	○	○	○
Grants or external funding (5)	○	○	○	○
Rely more on Document Delivery services (either InterLibrary Loan or Get It Now etc.) (6)	○	○	○	○

If other methods are used, please describe the method and indicate its importance.

_____

_____

_____

_____

Comments or Questions?

_____

_____

_____

_____

If you would like the results of this survey sent to you, please leave your email address here:

_____

_____

_____

_____

End of Block: Default Question Block

WIDE OPEN OR JUST AJAR? EVALUATING REAL USER METRICS IN OPEN ACCESS

Amy Brand
Director, The MIT Press, amybrand@mit.edu

Hillary Corbett
Director, Scholarly Communication and Digital
Publishing, Northeastern University Libraries,
h.corbett@northeastern.edu

Byron Russell
Head, Ingenta Connect, Ingenta, byron.russell@ingenta.com

Charles Watkinson
Associate University Librarian for Publishing, University of
Michigan Libraries, and Director, University of Michigan
Press, watkinc@umich.edu

Impact analysis has always been of great importance in academic publishing, as authors, publishers, and libraries seek return on their investments in research, time, and money. Open access is now an established component of the scholarly publishing landscape, but there are sometimes still misconceptions about the rigor (or lack thereof) of open access journals and presses, so it is especially important to be able to track and demonstrate the impact of open access publications. All key stakeholders in an open access environment need to understand what the full reach and significance of the published work *might be* (at the funding and peer review stages) and *actually is* (post-publication). How can success criteria and real impact be assessed when dealing with published open access material?

Once published, the value of open access content in terms of total impact over time is very difficult for librarians and publishers to evaluate. Simple volumetric assessment (downloads) is not nearly enough, of course, and is often not being reported to all stakeholders. And article-level metrics and citation counts may prove misleading without careful analysis. Additional complexities are the issues of reader behavior and their engagement with the work, and the social impact of open access content in nonacademic environments, such as high schools and the general public.

This chapter is derived from a panel presentation at the Charleston Conference in November 2017. It examines the issues and challenges surrounding the collection, management, and assimilation of usage data from three standpoints—authors (and by extension, publishers), libraries, and funders. It should be noted that while there are certainly many other types of open access material—technical reports, white papers, audiovisual material, and so on—we will focus here primarily on journals and books produced by scholarly publishers.

OPEN ACCESS METRICS: THE AUTHOR AND PUBLISHER PERSPECTIVE

The interests of authors and publishers are well aligned when it comes to wanting to measure the impact of their publications, whether open access or otherwise. For authors this goal has a personal dimension, because how their publications are cited and otherwise attended to has the ability to positively impact their academic careers, and librarians as well as publishers can support faculty in telling the story of their publications' impact.

Publishers tracking their open access publications typically observe immediate and rapid engagement with this content, in the form of views and download count as well as through altmetrics such as mentions on social media, in blogs, and on news sites. The MIT Press and the University of Michigan Press use the Altmetric platform to display these statistics to authors and their readers, for journal articles as well as books, whether open access or not. Altmetrics help authors track engagement with their publications beyond traditional citation metrics and therefore help demonstrate the reach these publications can have when made openly available. It is important to keep in mind, however, that altmetrics numbers do not necessarily communicate positive or negative reception of a title, particularly when it comes to social media; in some cases a title might be frequently mentioned on social media, for example, simply because it has an interesting or humorous title. So, deeper analysis of altmetrics beyond the total score is important, in order to assess meaningful usage such as inclusion of a title in a policy paper or a course syllabus.

Publishers can also observe an increase in downloads when a subscription journal switches to open access; however, download counts alone do not always tell a complete story of a journal's role in the scholarly literature. When the MIT Press journal *Computational Linguistics* transitioned from subscription-based to open access in 2009, its download counts shot up dramatically; the press also noticed increased readership of the journal in new regions such as Eastern Europe and China. But the download increase was not matched with a similar rise in impact factor, which is tied to citations, as shown in Figure 1—an indication that for open access journal articles, the correlation between downloads and citations is still not clearly understood. The MIT Press has anecdotally observed, though, that there is a correlation between downloads and citations for its open access books, and the number of books the press is making available open access has increased significantly in recent months in part due to a new relationship with the Internet Archive in which they are digitizing books from their deep backlist.

When it comes to books, print sales is another metric that is important to publishers and authors—even for open access titles. The MIT Press often sees significant print sales for the new open access titles it publishes. Some authors still demand substantial royalties (and advances) at the same time as they demand open access availability for their books, which necessitates a balancing act for publishers who may not yet have all the information needed to calculate the relationship between open access and sales.

Providing information to authors on how readers are engaging with their work can empower them to represent this in a variety of contexts. The MIT Press authors can subscribe via Altmetric to regular e-mails with updates on reader engagement as gathered through download statistics and altmetrics; authors can then use this data to enhance their online presence, such as through a Google Scholar profile or their NIH biosketch, and demonstrate the impact of their publications in their promotion and tenure portfolio. Beyond simple counts of downloads and mentions, publisher-provided metrics can help authors answer other important questions about their work,

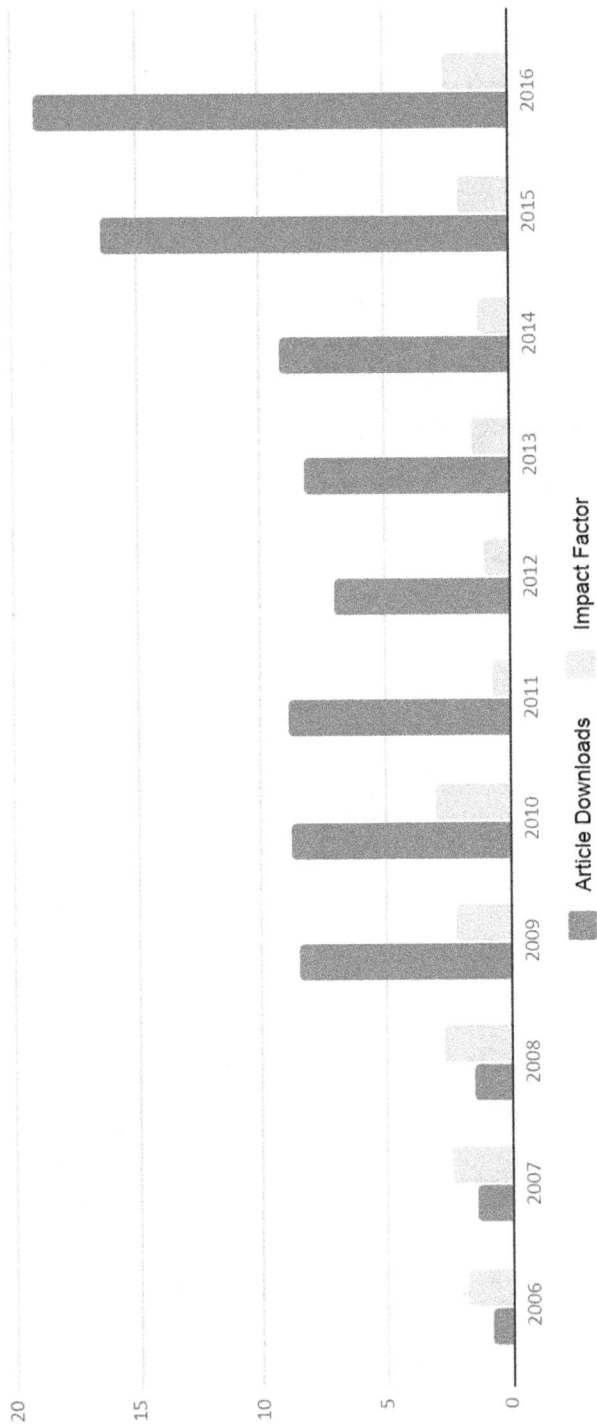

FIGURE 1. Article downloads and impact factor for *Computational Linguistics*, an MIT Press journal that switched to open access in 2009.

such as whether it is being read fully (some publishers measure time spent in an online book) and if it is reaching a global audience (through demographic data collected as part of web analytics gathered by the publisher). While these measures are available regardless of whether a publication is open access or not, the increased visibility and accessibility of open books and journal articles serve as a multiplier for the statistics that publishers can provide their authors.

WHAT DO LIBRARIES WANT TO KNOW ABOUT USAGE OF OPEN ACCESS MATERIALS? (AND WHY?)

Compared to subscription resources, it is very challenging for libraries to gauge usage of open access materials. When we pay for something, we expect to know how it is being used, and content providers meet that need through providing usage statistics and other metrics. And while usage of open access content is often also being tracked, that information typically tends to be used for internal purposes rather than being provided to libraries. There are a few exceptions, mostly where a payment is being made to support a service, like SCOAP3 or Knowledge Unlatched. But for the most part, little information is available about how users are engaging with open access content.

A further distinction between types of open access content can be made between wholly open collections that libraries support financially and the content found in hybrid journals, where subscription content is presented alongside open access articles funded through article processing charges (APCs). Libraries, or their institutions, may also fund articles published by their affiliated authors in open access journals that charge an APC, although many institutional open access funds exclude support for charges for publishing in a hybrid journal (on the principle that they are already financially supporting the journal through their subscription payments).[1] Article-level metrics in open access journals provide some sense of return on investment (ROI) for articles that libraries have funded through a membership discount or open access fund support for the APC, but it is not a 1-to-1 comparison—these metrics reflect everyone who has used the article, after all, not just an individual library's users. So the ROI becomes in part a measurement of altruism rather than of service to the library's users.

---

1. https://sparcopen.org/wp-content/uploads/2015/11/OA-Funds-in-Action_Nov-11-17.pdf

Where usage statistics are already being gathered and reported to libraries for subscription-based content, statistics for open access articles may also be provided. However, if a library does not subscribe to a hybrid journal, it would not receive any information about how its users are engaging with the journal's open content. For this and other open content where money is not changing hands, such as material found in repositories or on preprint servers, usage information could serve broader goals, such as learning more about users' information-seeking behavior, what types of sources users find valuable, and how libraries might realign collections strategies based on those insights. But how to get at this information is a puzzle yet to be solved.

There are several specific types of information that libraries would like to know about their users' engagement with open access content. For content published in traditional journals that the library does not subscribe to, are they accessing green open access versions of articles, archived in repositories or uploaded to preprint servers? Are they accessing gold open access content in journals that their library doesn't subscribe to? (And is the amount of content from the journals that they can access in this way adequate, or would they prefer that the library subscribe to all the journal content?) How are users engaging with content not formally published, such as dissertations and theses, white papers, and digital archival collections? Libraries supporting affordable course materials initiatives would also doubtless be interested to know if instructors are assigning openly available material as course readings.

Faculty use of open content in research can be tracked through citation analysis, but this is a very labor-intensive undertaking. Figure 2 illustrates such an assessment that was conducted for a subset of articles published at Northeastern University in 2014. The analysis reveals that almost half of the articles that these faculty cited in their own articles or conference papers were available open access—40% compared to 50% from journals that the Northeastern University Library subscribed to. If one assumes that citation indicates significant usage of an item (as opposed to the simple view or download), this is a very valuable insight, but the number of person-hours needed to distill this statistic out of the raw data makes the prospect of doing so on a larger scale and regularized basis daunting.

User behavior is also a complicating factor in getting an accurate and complete picture of how open access material is accessed. Libraries know that

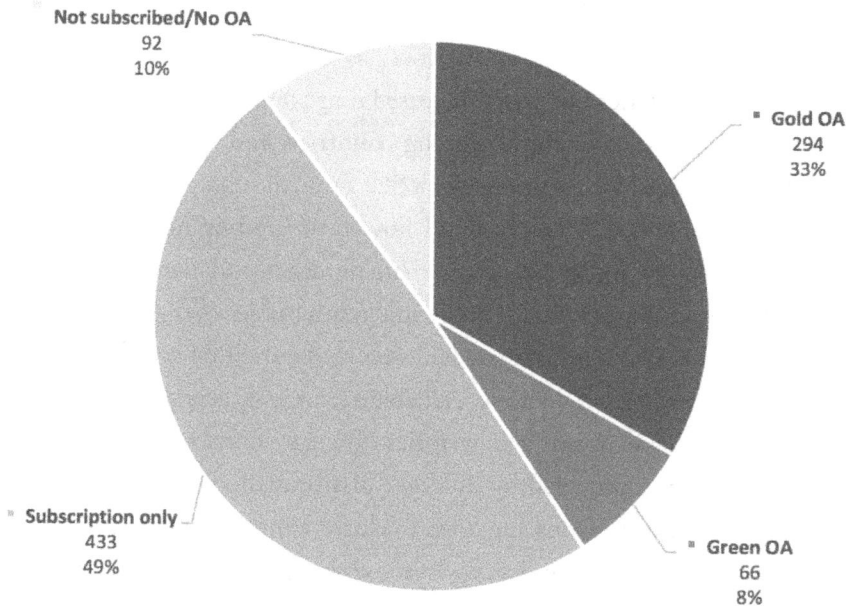

Source: Web of Science. Note: 119 self-citations were not counted as part of this data set.

FIGURE 2. Journal article and conference paper citations in 39 articles authored by Northeastern University College of Engineering faculty in 2014 (*n*=885)

many of their users start their literature search through Google or Google Scholar, rather than through the library's discovery system. If users run up against a paywall in their Google-based literature search, they often will try to obtain a free copy of the article through a variety of means that don't involve a library transaction. So, even where usage statistics are available, libraries can only track what gets accessed through their discovery system or link resolver.

WHAT DO FUNDERS WANT TO LEARN FROM OPEN ACCESS METRICS?

A diversity of funders, from government agencies and private foundations to universities, libraries, and individuals, support open access publishing. While they may have different motives for their support, they share common interests: they want to encourage use and reuse through open licensing of research outputs; they want to increase the reach of the work they fund for strategic and equity reasons; and they want to demonstrate impact and engagement.

Increased use and reuse through open licensing can be measured objectively through downloads or citation statistics, as compared with closed access materials; web analytics can reveal increased usage outside the academy, at less privileged institutions, or in developing countries; and impact and engagement can be gauged by mentions in policy forums, news media, and social media. Being able to tell stories about how their funding has accomplished these goals may be more important than numbers and data visualization, though this type of storytelling can be inherently subjective, and the ways in which funders measure impact is not always transparent or explicit.

A certain bluntness of the tools available at funders' disposal presents challenges in gathering data and telling stories. There is some lack of comparability in the reporting provided by different platforms, for example, as well as the basic challenge of comparing open to closed content when the individual works may have different audiences. In some cases, university privacy policies restrict the ability to see even aggregated behavior from users with particular characteristics that might be of interest. Storytelling has a natural affinity for qualitative rather than quantitative data, but it is difficult to ask individual users to share how an open access work has affected them.

At the University of Michigan Press, a strategic conversation is ongoing about how open access should be supported, particularly with regard to monograph publishing. Data available on efforts already under way shows a clear advantage to open access publishing: views and downloads of press books available open access through JSTOR are substantially higher than subscription-access titles, and their usage at less-resourced institutions and in geographically and economically diverse parts of the world is significant. Some images of these impacts are provided in Figures 3 and 4. In Figure 3 use on JSTOR of open access titles versus closed access titles from the University of Michigan Press in the first few months after the launch of the OA collection is shown. Novelty may have influenced the very high ratios of views and downloads. These have now settled down somewhat, but it is still the case that use on JSTOR (counting both chapter views and downloads) is around 20 times greater for open versus closed access books. In Figure 4, it is striking that open access books on JSTOR seem to be disproportionately downloaded by institutions in the developing world, by high schools, and by community colleges. This is exactly the sort of "open access advantage" one might hope to

Views per book per month

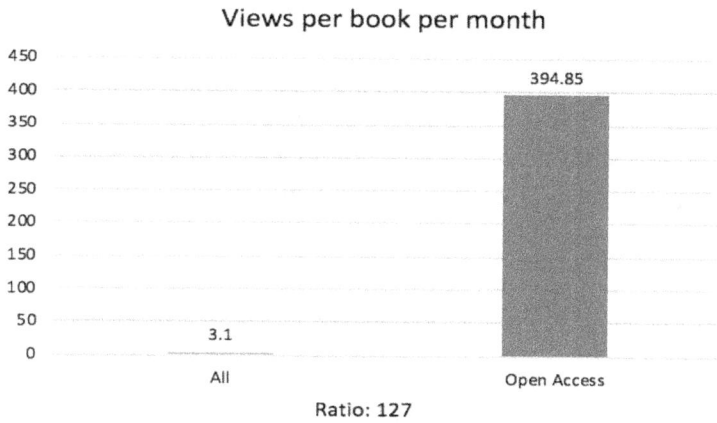

450
400 — 394.85
350
300
250
200
150
100
50
3.1
0

All   Open Access

Ratio: 127

Downloads per book per month

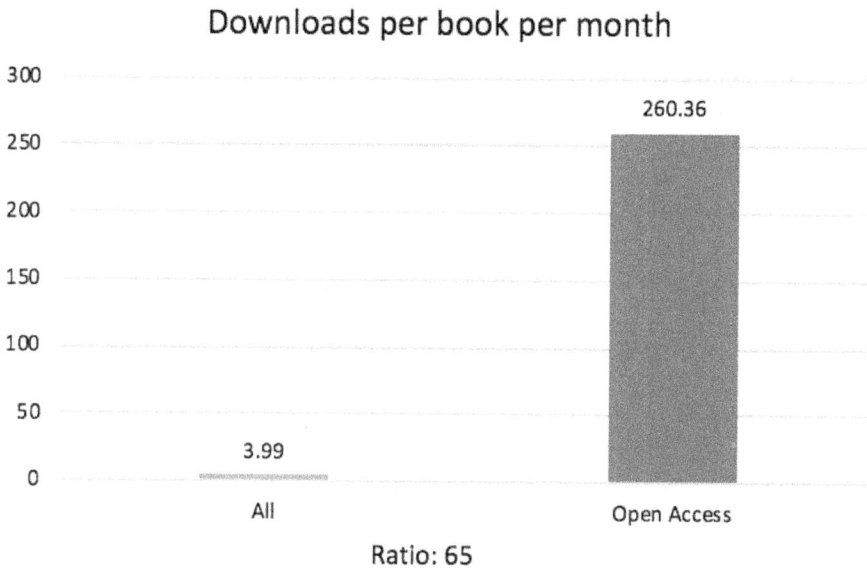

300
250 — 260.36
200
150
100
50
3.99
0

All   Open Access

Ratio: 65

FIGURE 3. Usage of University of Michigan Press titles available in JSTOR, October–December 2016

see, with books that otherwise may have been financially out of reach apparently receiving fairly heavy use from previously disenfranchised readers.

As described earlier, like the MIT Press, the University of Michigan Press uses Altmetric to display engagement with all its open access books on its own platform. Information gathered by Altmetric can be provided to external funders to help them measure the success of their support and tell their stories as well, for example, news media usage of a title on campaign finance reform for which open access was funded by the William and Flora Hewlett Foundation.

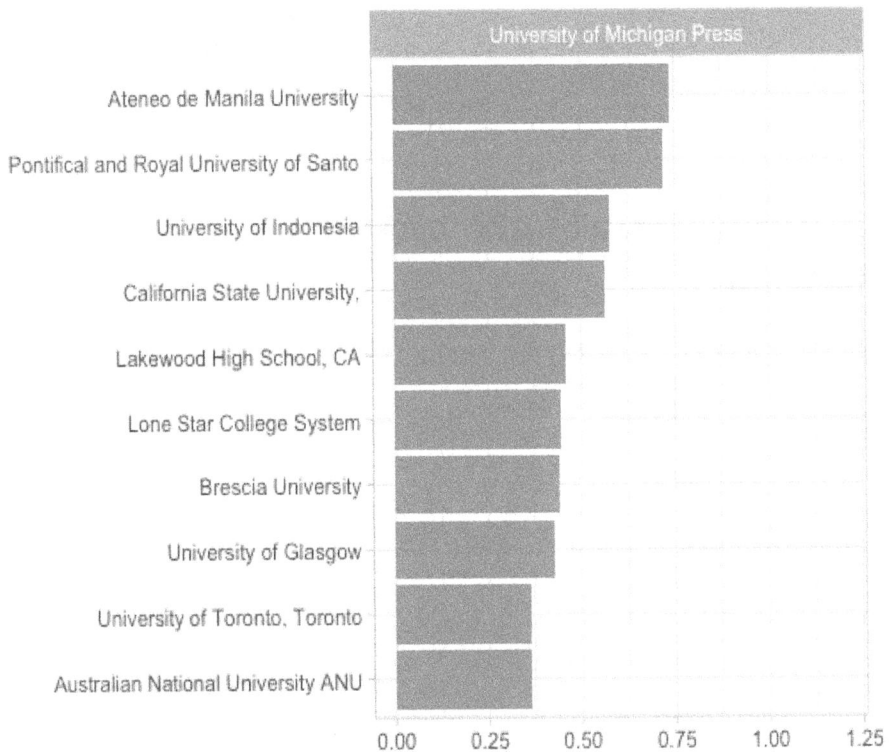

FIGURE 4. University of Michigan Press OA books on JSTOR: Top 10 institutions by total chapter views and downloads, according to publisher; and map of total chapter views and downloads by country (October 2016–July 2017)[2]

---

2. http://www.kuresearch.org/PDF/jstor_report.pdf

rank
[0, 3)
[3, 5)
[5, 11)
[11, 23)
[23, 49)
[49, 82)
[82, 128)
[128, 289)
[289, 502)
[502,33550]
NA

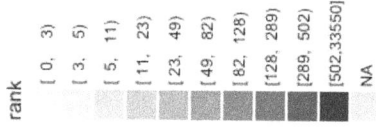

FIGURE 4. Continued

CONCLUSION

Clearly, there is still significant opportunity for growth and improvement in how usage of open access material is measured and assessed. And further research is still needed on the relationship between usage and citation of open access works—while overall a higher citation rate may likely be attributed to open access works, there are confounding factors.[3] Traditional measures of research impact such as the h-index may not accurately capture the extent to which open access journal articles are being used; because so much usage of open access material takes place outside the realm of traditional scholarship, it is difficult to measure completely and accurately. Altmetrics are certainly important in gauging usage both quantitatively and qualitatively, but what is the signal-to-noise ratio in an environment where increased downloads may be the result of what could be termed insignificant usage—such as social media mentions of an article with a quirky title? This can be challenging for authors who need to make a case for their open access publications in their promotion and tenure portfolios, and can potentially serve as a disincentive for publishing open access.

Libraries want to learn more about their users' information-seeking behaviors and how they make use of what they find openly available, but commonly run up against the limitations of how to gauge usage of such materials. While citation can indicate significant usage, it is extremely time consuming to conduct the in-depth citation analyses that will reveal this usage. Institutions that offer open access funds to support their authors' article processing charges may wish to calculate a return on investment in terms of a funded article's impact, but this is difficult to capture accurately due to the limitations of open access metrics.[4] External funders are also certainly interested in gauging the impact of their financial support, although sifting through usage data to produce narratives that demonstrate the value of a project they've funded can be time consuming, too. While publishers may report usage information to

---

3. Ottaviani, J. (2016). The Post-Embargo Open Access Citation Advantage: It Exists (Probably), It's Modest (Usually), and the Rich Get Richer (of Course). *PLoS ONE*, 11(8), e0159614. DOI: https://doi.org/10.1371/journal.pone.0159614

4. Hampson, C., & Stregger, E. (2017). Measuring Cost per Use of Library-Funded Open Access Article Processing Charges: Examination and Implications of One Method. *Journal of Librarianship and Scholarly Communication*, 5(1), eP2182. DOI: http://doi.org/10.7710/2162-3309.2182

their authors and funders, this is provided on an individual basis—there is no infrastructure in place for publisher/provider reporting on overall and title-level usage specifically of open access material to libraries. Development of a platform-agnostic tool or methodology to streamline reporting on usage of open access material would benefit all stakeholders.

Ultimately, we may be using the wrong terminology to describe what we are after. Is "metrics" a concept better suited to measuring the usage of materials where access is controlled? Like impact factor or the h-index, will our traditional, agreed-upon definition of metrics always fall short of ever accurately capturing the full picture? Perhaps "indicators of engagement" is a more appropriate way of describing the varied and sometimes unexpected ways in which open access publications are used, and a more useful way of framing the information that stakeholders hope to obtain about these materials.

www.ingramcontent.com/pod-product-compliance
Lightning Source LLC
Chambersburg PA
CBHW081249040426

42452CB00015B/2762